EARLS COURT

AND
OLYMPIA

FROM BUFFALO BILL
TO THE 'BRITS'

JOHN GLANFIELD

SUTTON PUBLISHING

for Caroline, Lucy, Amanda and my grandchildren

First published in 2003 by
Sutton Publishing Limited · Phoenix Mill
Thrupp · Stroud · Gloucestershire GL5 2BU

British Library Cataloguing in Publication Data
A catalogue record for this book is available from the British Library.

ISBN 0 7509 2998 7

Front endpaper: John Whitley's exhibition grounds, Earls Court, 1887. *(GHL, Illustrated London News, April 1887)*
Rear endpaper: Olympia, c. 1920. *(Simmons Aerofilms)*

Typeset in 10½ /14½pt GillSans Light
Typesetting and origination by
Sutton Publishing Limited.
Printed and bound in England by
J.H. Haynes & Co. Ltd, Sparkford.

CONTENTS

'I can assure you that any other combination of labours I may hereafter undertake will appear to me easy in comparison with that of organising the National Exhibitions at Earls Court.'

John R. Whitley, Director-General of the
National Exhibitions, London, 1892

ACKNOWLEDGEMENTS

SPECIAL THANKS must first go to Andrew Morris at Earls Court and Olympia. His generous and steadfast support opened numerous doors and, crucially, ensured the inclusion of many of the illustrations. I am also indebted to his colleagues Debbie Thomas for her invaluable and enthusiastic collaboration, and Vinesh Panchal whose patience and travels unearthed late treasure.

Of those who helped so willingly with research, guidance and timely encouragement I am particularly grateful to Jane Kimber, Borough Archivist for the London Borough of Hammersmith and Fulham and her colleagues Anne Wheeldon and Francis Serjeant, with all of whom it was a real and fruitful pleasure to work.

Sincere thanks also to Keith Whitehouse, Chairman of the Fulham and Hammersmith Local History Society, and Arthur Smith of Fulham, both of whom gave generous access to their extensive collections; and to local residents Rose O'Farrell and Anne Phillips who kindly provided personal recollections. I must thank Rachel Double and the Hammersmith & Fulham Gazette for these invaluable contacts.

Grateful thanks for research assistance goes to the staffs of the Humanities Rooms at the British Library, the Guildhall Library, London Metropolitan Archives, Royal Borough of Kensington and Chelsea Library, Eleanor Gawne at the RIBA, Ms Coi Gehrig of Denver Public Library, Colorado, Mary Green of Bay City, Michigan, the indefatigable Glenn Hatch and James Edmundson of News International, David Sheppard of the Daily Mail Picture Library and Danny Howell of Atlantic Syndication, and Emma Campbell of The Independent. Bill Tonkin, Secretary and Editor of the Exhibition Study Group, provided valuable information on Imre Kiralfy.

For event information and photos, many thanks to John Turner (circuses), Dan Gorton, James and Simon Brooks-Ward and Valerie Pedley (Olympia Showjumping Championships); Emma Kendrick-White, Pippa Roberts and Leslie Weller (Olympia Fine Art & Antiques Fair); Rebecca Macfarlane and Mark Bellamy (Royal Smithfield Show); Tom Nutley and Leonard Pearcey (World Travel Market); Jennifer Shelley (Montgomery Exhibitions); Rebecca Phillips (London Boat Show); Lisa Anderson and Sarah Sinclair (The BRITS Awards); Sue Baker (International Direct Marketing Fair); Dawn Milroy and Julian Graves (Amusement Trades Exhibition International); and Alistair Burtenshaw (London Book Fair). Joanne Davis in Hong Kong supplied Olympia Fashion Show photos, and Caroline Cousins provided stirring recollections of those days.

It would be impossible to draw a line in naming others at Earls Court and Olympia who gave such willing help. My sincere thanks go to them all including Brian Brown, Chris Morrison, Janet Smith, Barry Earl, Frank Henderson, Tony Hawkins, Alfie Sallis, John Dunstan, Michelle Walburn, Angela McNaught and Neil Davis.

Thanks also to Donovan White, Steve Phillips and Lorraine Choat of Trident Photo Services, London E14 for superb reproduction work, and to Clive Plant of Reproprint, Guildford for meticulous scanning. Photo recovery expert Ven Dodge again transformed ruinous images to printable condition, as for a previous tank history, for which I am most grateful.

Sarah Moore was again my wise and most welcome editor at Sutton, and grateful thanks goes also to Martin Latham for wrapper wizardry, and to Michelle Tilling. My last salute — the most heartfelt — is to Caroline my wife whose forbearance and good humour kept the show on the road.

Picture Source Abbreviations

AC   Author's collection
ECO   Archives, Earls Court & Olympia Group Ltd
GHL   Guildhall Library, City of London
H&FA   Hammersmith & Fulham Archives & Local History Centre
RBKC   Library, Royal Borough of Kensington & Chelsea

INTRODUCTION

WE PROBABLY TAKE THE EARLS COURT AND OLYMPIA show centres pretty much for granted. Like London's red buses, green parks and black cabs they have been part of the landscape for years. But consider what lies behind their looming bulk. Here are historic palaces of infinite variety, revolving doors through which much of our national life in work and play is reflected in the constant stream of events.

Dramatic spectacle has gripped – even shocked – Earls Court and Olympia audiences since the cowboy thrills of Buffalo Bill and Roman chariot races first drew them there in 1886/7. Long before the present Earls Court was built, vast shows on the site ran for five or six months at a time. Two million or more flocked to see them each year. Rival productions in Olympia's great arena were so lavish that more than once they broke the company. Events from Royal Tournaments to 'Grand Opera' have enthralled generations at the two centres, while trade exhibitions bring the world to the capital.

Here is the story of the pioneers of these hugely ambitious venues, and the showmen and impresarios who staked their shirts and reputations on productions so epic that they are unrepeatable today. We will join the audiences (and go behind the scenes) through constantly changing fashions in entertainment and the infinite demands of exhibitions to the present day.

All who work at the two halls, and those who organise and build the events, perform, exhibit or visit, are continuing a tradition which now spans three centuries. Applause, laughter and the music of a thousand shows hang indefinably in their cavernous and rarely silent air.

This is a story of crowds and colour, enterprise, courage – and disaster.

ONE
EARLS COURT
Revels & Riot

'For any leading London or southern athlete to receive civility, let alone favour from the owner of Lillie Bridge [Athletics Ground] is a thing seldom heard of.'

'It is not desirable to include in this [Athletic] Association [any] clubs who admit as members men who are not gentlemen by position or education.'

Walter Rye (1843–1929), pioneer of English athletics, during internal struggles for control of Lillie Bridge Athletics Ground, Fulham, 8 November 1871

PRINCE ALBERT'S GREAT EXHIBITION opened on 1 May 1851, captivating an entire generation and introducing an avalanche of decorative goods and manufactures from around the world. However ghastly and over-ornamented much of the Great Exhibition's 10 miles of exhibits may seem to the modern eye, the event stamped new standards of respectability and taste on the British domestic scene at the time, principally on an increasingly affluent and expanding middle class. It inspired the later mammoth shows which would combine mass entertainment with mass enlightenment. Prince Albert had lit a fuse that was to spark a trail of exhibitions across South Kensington before exploding spectacularly at Earls Court in 1887 – the year of his Queen's Golden Jubilee.

Meanwhile, Londoners continued to seek their thrills in Chelsea's Cremorne Gardens in Kings Road where there was always something novel to see. In the year of the Great Exhibition a big water fête was staged there, culminating in the blowing up of an obsolete warship. Balloon ascents from its 12 acres of pleasure grounds were accompanied by daring acrobats performing on trapezes slung from the passenger baskets. The sensational Leotard was one such acrobat-aviator of the 1860s. Parachute descents and pyrotechnics added to the adrenalin rush. Cremorne had opened some twenty years before as a sports ground. It soon expanded to supplant the notorious and declining Vauxhall Gardens, becoming instead the fashionable place to promenade along gas-lit paths, to dance, eat and maybe get a little drunk under open skies, away from the taverns and street hazards of a seedy West End.

The public appetite for sensation drove Cremorne's promoters to stage dramatic stunts such as a high-wire crossing of the Thames in 1861 by 'The Female Blondin', and a shambolic attempt to reproduce the famous Eglinton jousting tournament of 1839. Unfortunately the eclectic mix of circuses, equestrian events and even ballet became

Opposite: Amateur Cycling Championships 25-mile race on the cinders at the Lillie Bridge Athletic Ground, February 1875. *(H&FA)*

increasingly troubled by hooliganism, until Cremorne lost its licence and closed in 1877.

Less than a mile away the Lillie Bridge Athletic Ground had opened in March 1869. It is the first direct link with the present Earls Court Exhibition Centre nearby, which purchased the 7.5-acre site in the 1980s and today operates it as the 700-space Seagrave Road car park.

Until the 1820s the whole district was covered with small farms and market gardens. By the 1860s the countryside surrounding Earls Court was already pitted with brickfields for the new streets of houses which had crossed Kensington in a westbound tide and were about to engulf the hamlet. The surrounding street plan had been fully established in 1875 and was almost entirely built up. Earls Court took its name from the De Vere family, who were granted the Manor of Kensington after the Norman Conquest. Later, the head of the family was created Earl of Oxford. His manorial court stood beside a lane still called Old Manor Yard, though the court building was pulled down in 1886. The manor and its lands passed into other hands in 1610.

The Lillie Bridge Ground was operated by the Amateur Athletic Club (AAC) under the management of one John Chambers. It deserves to be remembered for some outstanding events, not least the second FA Cup Final in 1873. The first final had been played the previous year at Kennington Oval when Wanderers beat the favourites, the Royal Engineers. The following season they faced challengers Oxford University. Wanderers exercised their right to name the ground and Lillie Bridge saw their victory. Kick-off was delayed by thirty minutes to enable all concerned to watch the University Boat Race taking place nearby.

The rival London Athletic Club (LAC) was forced to swallow its considerable pride and hire the AAC's Lillie Bridge facility for its meetings, the track there being vastly superior to London's other running grounds. Soon, humiliated beyond endurance, the LAC launched a bid to overthrow Chambers and the AAC, take over its stronghold at Lillie Bridge and so gain control of the annual English Athletics Championships. Membership was the key. The London club relaxed its strict 'gentlemen only' rule to boost numbers. The athletics scene in those days was riddled with social prejudice. When the committee accepted tradesman William J. Morgan – a future champion – into membership in 1872, sixty members resigned in protest.

The 'gentleman amateur' die-hards of the LAC were led by 29-year-old Walter Rye, an acerbic lawyer whose weekly column in the *Sporting Gazette* nailed his victims to the floor. His comments on another athlete, winner of five rival AAC championships, are eye-wateringly candid: 'To a certain extent a champion is public property, and I should not be doing my duty if I did not point out that the systematic giving way to habits of inebriation must tell its tale sooner or later, especially on a constitution already undermined by venereal disease.' Of John Chambers Rye wrote: 'For any leading London or southern athlete to receive civility, let alone favour from the owner of Lillie Bridge is a thing seldom heard of.' Chambers certainly ran a tight ship. When the Fulham Fever Hospital was built by the Metropolitan Asylums Board in 1876 on the southern boundary of the Lillie Bridge ground, he insisted that his clientele should not have to suffer sight of the poxy inmates, nor they of his events. The hospital's boundary wall was accordingly topped by an enormous screen along its entire length. The site is now an ambulance station.

The London club pressed on, however, and slowly its membership broadened. By 1876 the still elitist AAC was on its knees, a prevailing joke being that it was down to three members – John Chambers, the pony and the roller. Chambers diversified. Ballooning had literally taken off in novelty and popularity by 1880 when the Balloon Society of Great Britain was formed. On its first anniversary the society held a Balloon Garden Party at Lillie Bridge. To the accompaniment of the band of the Scots Guards, on a windy and overcast July afternoon, the society's No. 1 balloon with a newly designed fabric and rubber envelope was inflated before a large and expectant crowd. The intention was to tether it as a captive craft for short ascents. The wind proved too strong, so the idea was abandoned in favour of a full launch and departure. The flying party of three included a youthful Mr Baden Powell, later the founder of the Boy Scout movement. They covered 25 miles, vastly amusing the inmates of the Essex County Lunatic Asylum beside which they (nearly) landed.

Sporting promoters had only to match two champions to be sure of big gate money and heavy betting. One such match produced one of the great performances of the century in August 1886. Wiltshireman Walter George had been Britain's champion long-distance runner for the past five years, breaking world records in the process and beating the best amateurs in the US and UK. One challenge remained – could he beat William Cummings, the best professional miler in the country?

George had to turn professional before the two could race. Because he worked long hours in a chemist's shop much of his training entailed running on the spot behind the counter, knees lifted high. He called it his 'hundred up' exercise. Came the day at Lillie Bridge, and an estimated 30,000 people turned out to watch the event. An eyewitness said that to avoid being mobbed George reached his dressing room at the top of the old grandstand by means of a ladder from the adjoining coal yard. The hard-fought race ended with his victory in an astounding 4 minutes 12.8 seconds. George

Oxford & Cambridge Athletic Sports 1-mile race at Lillie Bridge, March 1869. Note grounds manager Chambers' screen across Fulham Fever Hospital. Seagrave Road is behind the pavilion which was later burned down in a riot. (H&FA)

had beaten the world record by nearly 6 seconds. Cummings collapsed 60 yards short of the line. The world record set that day at Lillie Bridge remained unbroken by amateur or professional for twenty-nine years.

A less uplifting meeting in September 1887 ended with a riot, the burning down of the grandstand and a man's death. Harry Hutchens of Putney had been matched with Henry Gent of Darlington for the English professional championship over 120 yards, and £200. It attracted enormous interest and heavy betting. The 32-year-old Hutchens was thought unlikely to hold the very swift younger man. Coincidentally the backers in each camp engaged the same man, Ransome, a first-class sprinter, to run a trial against each contestant very shortly before the match. The results left Gent trailing.

No word of this reached the 6–7,000 spectators who awaited the 5 pm start. As these events customarily began later than scheduled in order to maximise gate receipts the crowd remained in good humour. But at around 5.45 the bookmakers changed their cry. Odds on Gent crashed from 3–1 as favourite to 10–1 against, followed shortly by offers to wager the cancellation of the race. At this, and still with no sign of the runners or word from the promoters, the mood quickly changed. The bookies made off and a section of the crowd rushed the ticket offices to demand refunds. Other infuriated punters chased the bookmakers into Lillie Bridge Road and, according to a report next day in *The Times*, so hung themselves about their departing cabs that the horses in their shafts were lifted off the ground.

Finding the offices closed and empty, numbers set to work to get their money's worth in damage. They fired the large veranda-fronted pavilion and continued on the side stands. While these burned they uprooted the tall flagstaff in the centre of the ground and used it as a battering ram to demolish more structures. With little left standing, the mob turned indiscriminately on the adjoining and unrelated Lillie Bridge concert hall on the north-east corner of the ground close to West Brompton railway station. Ironically, it was advertising an 'assault of arms' for later that evening – and it certainly received one. An unfortunate reporter on the roof was bombarded with bottles, broken chairs and palings while the rioters stacked timber against the wall for firing. The few police present managed to frustrate this. As the flames in John Chambers' wooden structures merged into a conflagration, columns of Bobbies with drawn truncheons arrived to try to restore order in a series of running fights.

The real tragedy lay in the death of Bill Coombs, a railway inspector at West Brompton, who suffered a heart attack while challenging rioters on the tracks. The Lillie Bridge ground never recovered from the incident and was closed down some months later. It was taken over by the London & North Western Railway Co. and used as a goods and coal station, into which they ran spurs. Meanwhile, a vast new enterprise directed at more decorous public education and tasteful entertainment had opened earlier that same year and was attracting vast crowds – just across the road.

TWO

EARLS COURT
Buffalo Bill

'We hear that the cowboys are wonders,
And do what rough riders dare,
So wherever the "pitch" is in London
Its wild horses will drag us there.
O, fancy the scene of excitement!
O, fancy five acres of thrill,
The cowboys and Injuns and horses,
And the far-famed Buffalo Bill!'

'The Referee', 1887

'I can assure you that any other combination of labours I may hereafter undertake will appear to me easy in comparison with that of organising the National Exhibitions at Earls Court.'

John R. Whitley, Director-General of the National Exhibitions, London, 1892

AS THE LILLIE BRIDGE ATHLETIC GROUND declined into disrepute and closure, a spectacular extravaganza was taking place on the opposite side of Lillie Road. Visualise a box of waste ground 600 yards or so square with Lillie Road across its base. Kensington's Warwick Road forms the right-hand boundary to the east and Fulham's North End Road is its western flank. The box was once farmland and orchards, bisected top to bottom in 1828 by the newly dug Kensington canal, an unprofitable venture which was cut from a point close by today's Olympia (just north of our box) straight down to the Thames at Chelsea Basin. A cholera outbreak later forced the closure of the canal as a public health hazard. It was infilled and overlaid by the West London Extension Railway in 1863 to link rail networks on either side of the Thames.

This north–south axis was and is the borough boundary between Kensington in the east and Hammersmith and Fulham opposite. Olympia is directly attached to it at the top end in Hammersmith, and today's two Earls Court halls sprawl across the axis at the bottom of the box, one hall in each borough. The waste ground was acquired in the 1860s by the Metropolitan District Railway Company, which quickly built West Brompton station on Lillie Road. Earls Court station followed in 1871 (it burned down four years later and was rebuilt on the other side of Earls Court Road, as now). The whole of our box soon became a cat's cradle of railway lines, sidings and wagon sheds operated by five railway companies.

Into this singularly unpromising real estate came bearded Yorkshireman John Robinson Whitley (1843–1922). As manager of his father's Leeds engineering works he had displayed their products at numerous continental exhibitions, becoming familiar with local commercial procedures and fluent in French, German and Italian. His experience led fifty British companies to invite him to represent them at the Paris exhibition of 1878. Soon afterwards ill-health from overwork forced Whitley's retirement from the family business. He sought new opportunities in travel.

The break came in New York in April 1884. Whitley learned that a group of American businessmen planned to organise an exhibition of the arts, manufactures and products of the Americas to be held the following year in London. He offered his services on condition that the show was confined to exhibits from the United States, a radical departure from the customary international format. Their cautious agreement was followed by prodigious labour. Whitley calculated that by the time the show opened he had read 27,000 letters, most of which required an answer, as well as making several more Atlantic crossings. Through his US contacts Whitley enlisted the active support of the new President, Grover Cleveland. An Anglo-American 'cabinet' was formed to give strategic direction and to secure the full participation of arts and industry, but no financial backing was forthcoming from the American government.

The American Exhibition was to open in London on 1 May 1886, running concurrently with a British Colonial and Indian Exhibition in nearby South Kensington. Whitley's rather unconvincing justification for this clash, supported by *The Times*, was that otherwise the American nation, a one-time colony, would be alone among the English-speaking races in not being represented in the capital of the mother country at that time. Besides, he argued, the two great events together would prove an irresistible draw, doubling the opportunity for enjoyment by the public and uniting American sellers with Eastern buyers for the first time ever. The Prince of Wales was closely associated with the Colonial and Indian Exhibition and made his considerable displeasure known through intermediaries only five months short of Whitley's May opening. Whitley and his associates capitulated, postponing their exhibition for twelve months to May 1887.

The royal intervention raised diplomatic issues. It brought President Cleveland's resignation as honorary president of the exhibition and further undermined confidence in Whitley's ability to deliver the show. Some key American supporters and exhibitors pulled out. Whitley had only just selected the Earls Court site, a perilously late decision had he kept to the 1886 opening. He still had to secure a lease of it from

John R. Whitley, pioneer of the Earls Court exhibition grounds. His inaugural American Exhibition opened on 9 May 1887. (AC)

James Forbes, canny chairman of the Metropolitan District Railway, which owned most of it, and from the Midland Railway for the rest. Both were reluctant to deal with him in such a shaky enterprise. Meanwhile, doubts and defections across the Atlantic threatened the exhibition's total collapse.

Fate threw Whitley a lifebelt while he was in Washington on a rescue mission. From his hotel window he saw a strange procession of savages and rough-riders on horseback leading wagons and mule trains. Impressed with this colourful display of American history and its crowd-pulling potential, he learned that Buffalo Bill's 'Wild West' had arrived in town. Next day in a muddy field he signed up Colonel William Frederic Cody – Buffalo Bill – and his show for its first European production.

Will Cody, pioneer, plainsman, pony express rider, expert tracker and heroic Indian fighter, got his nickname when he was hired by the builders of the Kansas Pacific Railroad to supply buffalo meat to feed the graders. He seems to have broken all records in managing to wipe out a large slice of the national herd, killing 4,862 buffalo in one year. In 1876 he accompanied the Black Hills expedition to avenge the massacre at General Custer's last stand. On reaching the Indian war party Cody rode out in front of the opposing forces and killed chief 'Yellow Hand' in single combat before the general engagement began. His general considered Cody's eyesight to be 'better than a good field glass'. His horsemanship and rifle shooting were unrivalled. Cody turned showman in North Platte, Nebraska, in 1883 with the first performance of his prairie pageant. For his London engagement he would receive a percentage of the gate receipts.

A full year passed in rebuilding confidence and commitment in America before Whitley was able to move on to the exhibition site at the beginning of January 1887.

Opposite: Colonel 'Buffalo Bill' Cody beside the Deadwood stagecoach. The English passengers look slightly nervous. Driver John Nelson is aloft. Because Nelson's right shoulder dislocated easily, he strapped his elbow to his belt to limit arm movement when cracking a whip. *(Denver Public Library)*

A group of cowboys work to settle a bucking horse in the Earls Court arena during a performance of the Wild West Show. Buffalo Bill Cody watches on a white horse. This shot was taken during the Show's return in 1892. Note the rooftops above the painted scenery *(Denver Public Library)*

Machinery gallery, American Exhibition, 1887. Note the hundreds of feet of powered shafting above the stands to drive exhibits. *(AC)*

Its 23 acres were spread across three irregular parcels of ground comprising cabbage patches and a large rubbish tip. They were effectively islands separated by railway tracks. Whitley had a bare four months to transform this derelict land into 8,000 sq. metres of covered exhibition space, a great arena, grandstands, gardens, pavilions, spectacular rides and amusements, together with all the infrastructure of public and back-of-house facilities, electric lighting, power generation and other technical services, groundworks, water, drainage, roads, footpaths, fencing and seven footbridges over the railways – all scaled to serve daily attendances of many thousands.

Throughout the showground one was never allowed to catch sight of a train. Railway lines and cuttings were hidden behind tall canvas screens painted annually with scenes from the subject country or theme. Where these included flower borders and shrubberies, real plantings were taken right up to the canvas. The *Survey of London* describes the grounds as being 'landscaped to give a superficial air of isolation'. Roof-tops and the chimney of the North End Brewery broke the spell.

The most easterly parcel fronting Warwick Road, now occupied by Earls Court 1, was a triangle surrounded by railways in shallow cuttings. It had been intended to accommodate Kensington Catholic Public School there, but the plan foundered in 1878 following allegations of financial irregularities and homosexual activities. The Wild West Show occupied this 12-acre 'Kensington triangle'. An arena a third of a mile in circumference was built. A covered grandstand seated 20,000 with standing room for another 10,000, and there were open terraces for 10,000 more. A painted backcloth depicting the Rocky Mountains encircled the other half of the arena at the Warwick Road end, the performers' access points cunningly disguised as dark clefts in the gorges. Behind the canvas-painted foothills towered a genuine mini-mountain peak of soil, rocks and trees. It took 10,000 cartloads of material to create, and a corduroy road of railway sleepers to get them there. The 'mountain' fortuitously hid the roof-tops from view in the grandstand. An encampment for the entire company filled the West Brompton corner of the triangle fronting today's entrance, with tepees for the Indians and cabins for the others.

A broad footbridge over the West London Railway's tracks linked the triangle to the central island, a narrow crooked north–south finger. The bridge was fully enclosed – and doubtless smoke-proof – and so draped and decorated with flowers and exhibits as to conceal its true purpose. It entered directly into the side of the exhibition hall, a cheap shed-like single-storey structure 1,140ft long and 120ft wide. Its frame was made

Earls Court exhibition grounds, 1894. Whitley's long exhibition building (centre) was replaced by the Empress Hall in 1896. The 'Gigantic Wheel' lay beyond it and was also completed that year. Earls Court I now occupies the triangle – note its big grandstand. (Crown copyright, Ordnance Survey 1894)

The sketch beneath clearly shows Buffalo Bill's arena and camp filling the triangle on the right where Earls Court I now stands. Note the covered grandstand seating 20,000. Shed-like exhibition galleries occupy the central 'island'. The Western Gardens lie beyond with a helter-skelter tower and switchback railway just visible. The artist has ignored the Midland Railway's unsightly sidings, preferring to show the area as a promenade! The depth of the forecourt fronting the exhibition buildings is exaggerated. Whitley had to build seven footbridges over the web of rail lines cutting across the site. (GHL, Illustrated London News, April 1887)

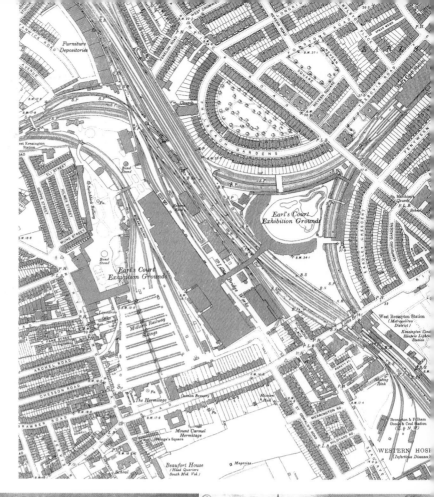

up from scrap rails, paired and bolted together as supporting columns, and roofed in corrugated iron and ribbed glass. Lines of flags hanging from almost every strut softened the interior. The hall lay end-on to a shallow forecourt entered from Richmond Gardens off Lillie Road. Its distinctly industrial saw-tooth gable ends were screened by a broad brick and stucco façade in classical style. 'Machinery in Motion' filled the back of the hall, its main feature being a 300hp Wheelock stationary engine under steam. Steam-powered shafting hundreds of feet long ran the length of the section to belt-drive a clattering array of agricultural and industrial exhibits.

Displays elsewhere in the hall covered mining, manufactured goods, science and education. Exhibits ranged from Gatling guns to false teeth, canned goods to jewellery, sewing machines to garden statuary. An annexe housed the main restaurant and behind it stood the Fine Arts building, a brick structure containing over 400 examples of American sculpture and painting, engravings and photography. Rothermel's dramatic 'Battle of Gettysburg', 36ft long and 16ft high, filled an entire wall. Ornamental gardens lay beyond, with an entrance at the tip of the 'finger' beside West Kensington station.

The central island was bridge-linked in turn to the third parcel, the Western Pleasure Gardens, largely set back from North End Road. Its 12 acres were planted with native North American trees, shrubs and flowers, with a switchback railway, toboggan slide and lesser amusements. Here also was Europe's largest bandstand where the Grenadier Guards played twice-daily.

Two gangs of a thousand men each worked twelve-hour shifts round the clock behind giant screens. Roofing the hall fell well behind schedule as difficulties arose in fitting the large sheets of glass. March brought heavy snow and more delay, forcing Whitley to take on a further 800 men. He had set up a works department under general foreman Edwin Smith of Estcourt Road, whose son and grandson followed him on the site over the next fifty-three years until the Second World War intervened. They typify a widespread tradition of continuity of service by local families through the generations at the Earls Court and Olympia centres which continued well into the 1970s. Edwin Smith's grandson Arthur, a sprightly octogenarian living close to today's Earls Court, recalls his father working on the showgrounds there for Edwin as carpenter and joiner, having started in 1900 at 11½d an hour for a fifty-hour week. Promotion to foreman brought him a rise to one shilling. Arthur's brother followed in the 1930s, working as an office boy until the war closed Earls Court.

The 42-year-old Colonel Cody had brought over a fair slice of the Old West including more than a hundred Indians – Sioux, Cheyenne, Kiowa, Pawnee and Ogallalla – with their squaws and children, none of whom had ever been off their reservations before joining the show. They were led by Chief Red Shirt, a formidable character who had recently quelled an uprising among his people stirred up by a usurper. Striding into the man's camp with two aides, he personally shot him dead. The voyage across the Atlantic in the 'great fire-boat' terrified and depressed the Indians. They contemplated the heaving expanse of ocean and lapsed into singing their death songs. The troupe also included 150 assorted cowboys, cattle herders and Mexican prairie riders with 170 bronco horses, Indian ponies and fearsome 'buckers'. They brought buffaloes, wild

Texas steers, mules, elk, deer, a dozen 'prairie schooner' wagons and, of course, the famous Deadwood stagecoach fresh from its last encounter with an Indian war party, or was it a bandit gang?

The Prince and Princess of Wales made a private visit a few days before the opening. The still unfinished Wild West site was semi-waterlogged after rain, the 7-acre arena a morass from haulage of heavy timbers. Cody's imperturbable reaction was to bless the gods of the plains for having 'struck a country where water is plentiful and the grazing good'! The prince and princess with their three daughters and a large entourage settled into the royal box for an exclusive performance. At a signal from the prince, the entire troop of cowboys, Mexican vaqueros and redskins charged at full gallop from concealment and raced whooping and yelling round the immense arena. This was no restrained theatrical performance – their blood was up. Thrilled, the royal party rose at the sight, Prince Edward leaning half out of the box. 'Cody,' the colonel mused to himself, 'you have fetched 'em.' By the end the royal party and performers alike were elated. The prince had remained standing – and often shouting enthusiastically for most of the ninety minutes.

On being presented to the Danish-born princess the young crack-shots Annie Oakley and Lilian Smith, quite carried away, each grasped her hand for a vigorous shake. The princess laughingly responded. A close inspection of the Indian camp and stables followed, the muddy ground notwithstanding. Princess Alexandra paid special attention to welfare issues, learning that the company consumed 6,000lb of fresh meat daily. Medical needs were met by an Englishman, the unfortunately named Dr Coffin.

On their departure the prince solemnly exchanged greetings with Red Shirt and presented him with the contents of his cigarette case.

The exhibition was officially opened on 9 May by its president, Colonel Henry S. Russell of Boston, on a day of sunshine and fleecy clouds. Minimal attention was paid to his address and when John Whitley rose to speak, inviting all present to join him in the further development of the New World, much of the crowd took him at his word and headed straight for the exits. Considerable building work remained unfinished behind the screening, and a glance at the exhibition galleries beyond the dais would have revealed semi-chaos with many half-built or empty stands. A special disappointment to Whitley was the large and magnificent model of Philadelphia's new city hall which had arrived in thirty-three carefully packed cases. After rough handling en route barely a quarter of it had been recoverable for display.

General order was achieved there within days, but most visitors headed the other way, across the bridge, to discover the mysteries of the Wild West. With no movies, television, travel opportunities or images of any kind save artist's impressions, most were totally unprepared for what lay ahead. *The Times* estimated the first day's attendance at 28,000, those without official invitations paying one guinea. Thereafter, daily admission between 10.30am and 10.30pm was one shilling, or two and sixpence to include a seat at the Wild West Show (which gave a ninety-minute performance twice-daily). One could stand in the amphitheatre for a shilling, take an unreserved covered seat for two shillings, pre-book a private box for four for twenty-five shillings,

John Whitley – cloaked, front centre – and Earls Court's senior staff. General foreman Edwin Smith perches far right. *(Arthur Smith collection)*

or for a party of six for thirty-five shillings. Once past the turnstiles, expectant visitors smelt and heard their first intimations of the West – a mix of horse and buffalo dung, and the laughing soft-spoken negros selling something called 'popcorn' in the stands: 'Pop-cohn! Pop-cohn! Keeps yeh cool, calm and kerlected throughout the puffohmance!'

Cody introduced his audiences to life on the prairie – how the mailcoaches were brought safely through the Indian frontier territories; how to ride bucking broncos; how to rope and ride wild Texas steers; how mounted horsemen could pick up objects on the ground at full gallop; how the Indians fought and danced; and much, much more. A London reporter recorded his impressions:

As we took our places in one of the little boxes which edge the arena, we could not help being struck by the effectiveness of the scene before us. The size of the enclosure was one element, and this was cleverly increased by the picturesque scenery which enclosed half of the circle. At the edge of the ash-covered arena were drawn up on parade the whole strength of the Wild West company. There were the various tribes of Indians in their war paint and feathers, the Mexicans, the ladies and the cowboys, and a fine array they made with the chiefs of each tribe, the renowned Sergeant Bates, the equally celebrated Buffalo Bill, the stalwart Buck Taylor, and others who were introduced by Mr Frank Richmond who, from the top of an elevated platform, described the show as it proceeded.

The post of lecturer is no sinecure when such a vast area has to be filled by the voice of the speaker; but Mr Richmond made every sentence distinctly heard, and the interesting information conveyed by him in a mellow and decidedly audible voice was one of the most agreeable features of the performance. Few of the audience would have remembered the history of the Pony Express, or the way in which the mails were carried. The emigrant train, which next wended its way across the arena with its teams of oxen and mules, its ancient wagons and their burden of families and household goods, to be attacked by a tribe of redskins, who were soon repulsed by the ever-ready cowboys, was an equally interesting resurrection of a method of peopling the soil practised even now in the remoter regions of the West.

The next sensation was created by Miss Lilian Smith the 'California Girl' whose forte is shooting at a swinging target. She complicates her feats by adding all kinds of difficulties to her aim, and her crowning achievements of smashing a glass ball made to revolve horizontally at great speed and clearing off ball after ball on the target just mentioned, to the number of twenty, were really marvellous. The part of the entertainment most novel to Londoners was undoubtedly the riding of the 'bucking' horses. As Mr Richmond explained, no cruelty is used to make these animals buck. It is simply 'a way they've got.' The ugliest of the lot was that bestridden at the conclusion of this part of the show by Antonio Esqueval, but they all showed what a rebellious demon there is in a half-broken horse who has lost his fear of man. The bucking horses should be seen by everyone in London who takes an interest in the 'noble animal.'

The attack on the Deadwood stage coach was a very effective spectacle and in this, as in the attack on a settler's homestead, there was a great amount of powder burnt. Mustang Jack performed the startling feat of clearing a horse sixteen hands high, having previously covered thirteen feet with a standing leap – an extraordinary jumper. Buffalo Bill's speciality is shooting whilst riding at full gallop, which he does to wonderful perfection. He is accompanied by an Indian bearing a basketful of glass balls which he throws high into the air, and Mr Cody smashes each with unerring aim whilst both horses are going at a hard gallop. The buffalo hunt was immensely realistic. There were other interesting feats; picking up handkerchiefs from the ground at full gallop, and similarly a trailing rope attached to a runaway horse; riding by two ladies in short races together, and between Indian boys mounted on mustang ponies. A Virginian reel danced on horseback. The show is certain to draw thousands.

He ended with a plea for the inclusion of 'a little scalping. Why should not the Indians overcome a party of scouts and raise their hair? Wigs and scalps are not very expensive and carmine is cheap.'

Next to Buffalo Bill in the nation's esteem was little Annie Oakley, twenty-seven years old and looking seventeen. She and her husband Frank Butler had evolved an

Annie Oakley in front of the settlers' log cabin in the Earls Court arena, 1887. (Denver Public Library)

amazing sharp-shooting routine. They began with clay pigeons. Frank released a single 4-inch clay while Annie, disdaining to hold a rifle at the ready, had to pick it up off the ground before aiming and always hitting the falling target. This was repeated with two, three, then four clays in the air together. Next, with a call for silence from Mr Richmond, Annie turned her back on Frank and, with the aid of a small mirror, shot a hole in the playing card held in Frank's outstretched hand. Annie would also push the muzzle of her rifle through a playing card to mask the sight before extinguishing a cigar held between Frank's gritted teeth at twenty paces. Her uncanny achievements brought many offers and she and Frank quit the show on its close at Earls Court, preferring a five-week booking in Paris and a personal invitation from Crown Prince Wilhelm ('Kaiser Bill') to give an exhibition shooting match in Berlin.

In the quieter Western Gardens the Welcome Club became a popular rendezvous for London's rank and fashion. Whitley shrewdly recognised the need to attract society, and introduced the comfortably appointed facility for a fee-paying membership restricted to 300 gentlemen. They received season tickets to the exhibition, attractive club badges and other privileges. Membership was strictly 'men only', ladies being admitted as their guests, for whom there was an adjoining Ladies' Pavilion. Behind the club's shady veranda a buffet dispensed American iced drinks. Afternoon tea was served on the lawn, where one could relax in big wicker chairs and listen to the band across the way. Garden parties became a regular feature. Later additions included a long garden shelter divided into dining alcoves with vines twining about the supporting pillars.

The site came into its own on summer evenings when myriad coloured electric lamps glowed across the exhibition grounds. Electric light was still a matter for wonderment. The central areas were lit by ten arc-lights of 10,000 candlepower apiece, with another 250 of 2,000 candlepower in the exhibition galleries and public rooms. The nightwatchmen made do with candles in their huts, burning 2lb nightly according to Whitley's accounts.

The 450ft switchback railway introduced the American roller-coaster to London. A tall six-track toboggan run with a vast slope of 16,000 sq. ft gave further opportunity for excitement, even hysteria. Canadian visitors were much taken with this, tobogganing being a novelty to most others. More genteel amusements were to be found elsewhere.

A letter from the palace was delivered to Earls Court two days after the show opened. It stated 'By command of Her Majesty, the Queen' that she wished to attend a private performance of the Wild West Show that same afternoon at 5pm. It was an

Queen Victoria at the Wild West Show, Earls Court, 1887. *Clockwise from top left:* The arena from an otherwise empty grandstand. Newly married sharpshooter Lillian Smith, aged sixteen, shows the Queen her rifle. The 'Great White Mother' is shown an Indian papoose. Chief Red Shirt is presented to Her Majesty, Colonel Cody behind. *(ECO)*

unexpected royal command which delighted the incredulous Bill Cody and left the establishment and much of the press gasping in disbelief. The reclusive queen was bestowing on a foreign entertainment the honour of her presence which, with only one recent exception, had been denied the British theatre or any other public event since the death of the Prince Consort twenty-six years before. There were two snags. As it was to be a private viewing the public would have to be excluded, and Victoria required to see everything in one hour. Already the grounds were filling in anticipation of the first performance at 3pm. It was too late to forewarn the thousands planning to attend that afternoon; only those with advance tickets to seats and boxes could be refunded but all would have a rare opportunity to see their queen.

Cody reworked the running order. The show so captivated Victoria that she rose in the almost empty grandstand and bowed deeply to the American flag when it was carried into the arena and introduced as an emblem of peace and friendship to all the world. Her gracious and undoubtedly spontaneous royal salute set the seal on Anglo-American accord, raising a great cheer from all in the arena, to be repeated by a huge crowd in Warwick Road on her departure.

Some English commentators initially wrote off the whole event as 'a mere tradesmen's exhibition', but most gave it high praise. The American Exhibition was not only a popular triumph, it soon became fashionable, a much more elusive achievement. It was routine for the surrounding roads to be choked with carriages and liveried footmen awaiting their passengers. Whitley had arranged for thirty-seven railway companies to lay on extra daily services with through tickets to Earls Court from all parts of the country. Employers and working men's associations could obtain certificates for artisan employees and members entitling the men to heavily discounted travel and admission tickets to the exhibition from any railway booking office within a 25-mile radius of Earls Court. A total of 600 trains arrived each day at the four stations close to the showground, where some platforms were lengthened and ticket offices enlarged. Earls Court, West Brompton and West Kensington stations actually fronted three of the event's five entrances.

A third royal command arrived, calling for a performance in June before half the crowned heads of Europe. They would be in London as the Queen's guests, and were to attend a solemn service of thanksgiving at Westminster Abbey on the following day as the climax of her Golden Jubilee celebrations. Victoria herself did not attend the show on this occasion but the Prince and Princess of Wales led arguably the most comprehensive royal party ever to honour a public entertainment – the Kings of Denmark, Saxony, Belgium and Greece, the Queen of Belgium, the Crown Princes of Austria, Germany, Norway and Sweden, Princess Victoria of Prussia, Prince George of Greece and numberless lords and ladies graced the show.

Cody recalled that the old Deadwood stagecoach, 'baptised in fire and blood' so often on the plains, had the honour of carrying four kings and the Prince of Wales that day during the attack by the redskins. Princess Alexandra led the boarding party, with Prince Edward riding on top beside Cody while young Prince Albert sat inside puffing cigarette smoke alternately into his mother's face and the King of Denmark's. Will Cody had instructed the Indians not to tone down their habitual display of scalp-hungry rifle-carrying savagery. They turned in a chillingly appropriate attack before the cowboys came to the rescue of the royals. Prince Edward, having just learned the rudiments of poker from Cody, remarked: 'Colonel, you never held four kings like these before'. Cody dryly replied that he had held four kings, 'but four kings and the Prince of Wales makes a royal flush, such as no man has ever held before'. The Prince burst out laughing before trying to explain the exchange in three languages to a bemused gathering of monarchs for whom 'poker' was synonymous only with 'fireside'. The party then went on to sample the switchback railway, the four kings sitting impassively and clutching their hats in defiance of unfamiliar g-forces while Alexandra screamed in delight and Prince Albert smoked on.

When the exhibition closed on 31 October after 151 days its turnstiles had clicked through 2.23 million visitors, the daily average approaching 15,000. Among them, at John Whitley's invitation, were all 500 masters and boys of Harrow school, his son being a pupil there at the time.

In an astonishingly frank, even bitter, valedictory address before a distinguished gathering of leading British and American industrialists and academics, Whitley bluntly accused the US government and press of wilful and destructive hostility:

Colonel Cody beside the tall and realistically painted canvas backdrop in Earls Court's arena during his show's return in 1892. (Denver Public Library)

This exhibition has been organised and conducted without either subsidy, assistance or even encouragement from the United States Government. 'All's well that ends well', and we can afford to be magnanimous to those persons who fiercely denounced and severely criticised the efforts of my colleagues and myself for three long years. There has even been a certain sense of additional satisfaction in carrying the Exhibition through to a successful issue in spite of misdirected opposition on the part of those who are supposed to mould public opinion in America, and of those who represent the Governmental functions of the United States in this country.

From this, our last meeting, we send a greeting of forgiveness and peace to those who endeavoured, but unsuccessfully, to crush the life out of our good work from the very hour of its birth.

The American Exhibition was a single-handed triumph for John Whitley, most powerfully aided by the presence of Will Cody and his show. In freely acknowledging this, Whitley nevertheless had mixed feelings that so many visitors had been diverted to the entertainment aspect of the exhibition. He resolved to rebalance future events – planning for the next show was already nearing completion.

Triumph in triplicate

Whitley's Italian Exhibition opened the following year on 12 May 1888. He had built two further halls in the Western Gardens which, together with the original main block, housed a cross-section of the industry and culture of that country. Needless to say the Fine Art galleries were an outstanding feature, but once again it was the arena that drew the biggest crowds. The grandstand seating had been carried right round to transform it into Rome's Colosseum; coincidentally the two arenas were almost identical in size. Audiences used only to the images of graphic artists were confronted for the first time in their lives with a stunning re-enactment of Roman games, gladiatorial combats, wrestling, thundering chariot races and triumphal processions. A section of the arena was built up to represent the serried tiers of seating and spectators in the original Forum, the front row of seats being filled with Whitley's employees in full costume, while behind them a vast canvas was painted with continued tiers of seated spectators in perspective. The effect was uncanny at a short distance.

Twice a day 20,000 people could sit or stand to watch the 500 performers, but there was a catch. After the runaway success of Buffalo Bill's show, which left the exhibition section trailing badly, Whitley held back the arena show for the first two months to ensure the exhibition received full attention. The exhibition ran for 148 days and drew 1,743,445 visitors, a daily average of 11,780.

Exhausted by his labours, Whitley took a break before returning to complete an astounding quartet with his 'French Exhibition' in 1890 and the 'German Exhibition' the following year, drawing attendances of 1.32 million and 1.37 million respectively. The indifference of the British government towards Whitley's efforts to foster international accord and trade turned to open hostility during the planning for the German event. He was shocked to find that the government had informed Berlin of its disapproval of the project, which it would not support. The German emperor declined to grant Whitley an audience because 'the German Exhibition which it is proposed to hold in London is not promoted by Her Majesty's Government'. The word ran back through German trade and industry that the event was best avoided. The potential disaster was averted by John Whitley's personal courage and integrity.

Whitley received no official thanks or honour from his own country for seven years of high endeavour and achievement. He claimed that he never made a penny, and there is no reason to doubt him. He later sought to further Anglo-French relations in some more lasting form, and was instrumental in founding a pleasure resort at Le Touquet. He was not entirely happy with the result, however, and moved on to acquire an estate near Hardelot which he successfully developed with high-class villas, a golf course and tennis courts.

Sunset?

Whitley's departure was followed by a period of great uncertainty during which the Metropolitan District Railway threatened to put a coal depot on the arena. It relented when promoters H.E. Milner and H.P. Dodson made enquiries, resulting in the

International Horticultural Exhibition which opened in May 1892, supported by a return of Bill Cody's Wild West Show for a run of six months. This was Cody's final engagement of a highly successful two-year European tour. In place of Red Shirt, Cody brought over as head chief Long Wolf, a Sioux warrior who had remained with the colonel since the 1887 Earls Court show. Long Wolf was believed to have taken part in the Battle of Little Big Horn and the defeat of Custer and the 7th Cavalry in 1876. Now he was part of its twice-daily re-enactment. Tragically, he succumbed within weeks to scarlet fever, which defied the efforts of the medicine man and Dr Coffin. The 59-year-old Long Wolf died in June and was buried across the road in the fashionable Brompton cemetery after a moving ceremony attended by his widow and the whole company. (Was Long Wolf really at the historic battle? The autopsy following his death records that his body was 'covered in gunshot wounds and sabre cuts'. Best leave it at that.)

Eight weeks later his grave was opened to receive 20-month-old White Star Ghost Dog, a little girl who had lost her life during a performance illustrating Indian life on the plains. Too young to walk, she had been placed in a saddlebag slung across a horse's back for a parade of the camp's children. She fell out, landing on her head. Her father, Ghost Dog, begged that she should be allowed to join Long Wolf rather than wander alone with unfamiliar spirits in a foreign land. The authorities approved. Their spirits journeyed together until their homecoming in 1997 when Long Wolf was laid to rest in his tribal burial grounds on the site of the massacre at Wounded Knee in South Dakota. His great-grandson, rancher John Black Feather, had brought them both back at last after a national appeal for funds.

Milner and Dodson went on to stage the Exhibition of Forestry and Gardening in 1893. It was much enlivened by Captain Paul Boyton's Aquatic Show. He flooded the old arena and built a tall water chute backing on to Lillie Road, precisely over today's West Brompton entrance to the Earls Court Centre. The water toboggan's sensational ride made it an immediate winner and it was retained for future shows.

But what shows? Milner and Dodson had left the scene. Although Earls Court was by now firmly established as a national treasure its gilt was beginning to fade. The temporary timber and corrugated iron buildings were starting to age and the harsh surroundings were hardly the stuff with which to build dreams. The railway landlords would not sink shareholders' money into the speculative reconstruction of a showground. It faced perhaps irreversible decline. Earls Court awaited a saviour.

Battle-scarred Long Wolf of Buffalo Bill's show died during the Earls Court season in 1892. An Indian baby also died and was buried beside him. They were carried home to Dakota's Black Hills in 1997. (*The Times*)

THREE

OLYMPIA
Boom to Bust

*'Each comer who chooses may sport with the muses
Or notice the uses of genius or skill,
And find the employment of means for enjoyment
In modern Olympia all wishes fulfil.'*

Mrs W.A. Barrett, 'Ode to Olympia', 1886

OLYMPIA'S STORY BEGAN in May 1884. While John Whitley anxiously awaited reaction from New York to his proposals for staging an American Exhibition in London, the National Agricultural Hall Company was formed with the aim of building and operating the country's largest covered show centre. The National Agricultural Hall was to present 'cattle, horse, poultry, dairy, dog and implement shows and other agricultural displays; national and international exhibitions, military tournaments, sports and theatricals; regular sales of livestock and carriages etc.' Mr J.S. Wood, its general manager, assured enquirers for bookings that 'there are already plenty of applications and we can accommodate all, so long as they are high in tone'. The hall was soon renamed Olympia in keeping with its ideals and objects:

> . . . To provide healthy amusement and reinvigorate by brilliant demonstrations the national love of athletic exercises and contests of skill; to raise the tone of popular taste by entertainments and displays which shall be of the purest and highest character; to educate the masses, aye, and even the 'classes' by exhibitions of art, science and industry.

The management confidently believed that the Grand Military Tournament and Assault-At-Arms (later the Royal Tournament) would transfer from the smaller Agricultural Hall in Islington to Olympia's giant arena and greater seating capacity. Its livestock shows were expected to follow sooner or later. The Islington hall is still going strong today as the Business Design Centre, fondly remembered by old timers as the 'Aggie'. Its owners acquired the Earls Court and Olympia centres in a bold move in 1999.

The Aggie had hosted the Tournament since its launch there in 1880. Its secretary, General E.S. Burnaby was said at the time to have originated the idea of the Olympia hall. He urged the Tournament's removal to a larger West End arena if one could be built, so that 'mimic warfare might be carried out with greater and more realistic effects than was possible in any existing hall'. The Tournament was financially weak and Burnaby had to boost attendances. The public in turn demanded mock battles on a grand scale, for which the Islington hall was too small. Burnaby's cry was taken up by the London press in 1884 when the National Agricultural Hall Company was formed, but the old general had been dead for nearly two years by then and the drive to expand the Tournament died with him. It marked time at Islington for another twenty-three years.

The National Agricultural Hall Company was chaired by the Earl of Lathom, the Lord Chamberlain. (He later secured a foothold in the Earls Court camp as a member of John Whitley's Exhibition Reception Committee.) 'Discreet and sober' Mr J.S. Wood, his first general manager, was an experienced event organiser, having produced an Old English Fair in South Kensington which took London by storm. A Shakespearean Show had followed. The new company was to be capitalised at £200,000, half of which was taken up privately in £10 shares, the balance being offered to the public. Lathom's next most pressing task was to find a location with good rail access.

West London was now the centre for the capital's exhibitions and grand events. Lathom found a prime site in Hammersmith – 6 acres and 37 perches of nursery grounds. The company bought the freehold from one E.L. Hunt in 1885 for £31,000 cash and a thousand £10 shares. The site lay behind a row of large houses comprising the West Kensington Gardens Estate, which fronted Hammersmith Road. In truth there was no such place as 'West' Kensington but developers applied the name to encourage sales. Addison Road station flanked the site on the east side, the line of the railway forming the borough boundary (John Whitley's Earls Court showground would be one stop away). Blythe Road, once Blind Lane, marked the western boundary. The nursery's northern extremity fronted the later Maclise Road. In 1885 it faced acres of brickfields.

Hammersmith Road was the turnpike to Brentford, forming part of the Great West Road. The Bell and Anchor public house stood on the Blythe Road corner in the present Olympia 2 car park. In the 1700s it was the Robin Hood alehouse, fronted by a tollgate across

The tollgate and keeper's house in Hammersmith Road beside the junction with Blythe Road which is immediately beyond. The tall Bell and Anchor pub stood in the corner of what is today's Olympia 2 car park. It was demolished after the Second World War. *(H&FA)*

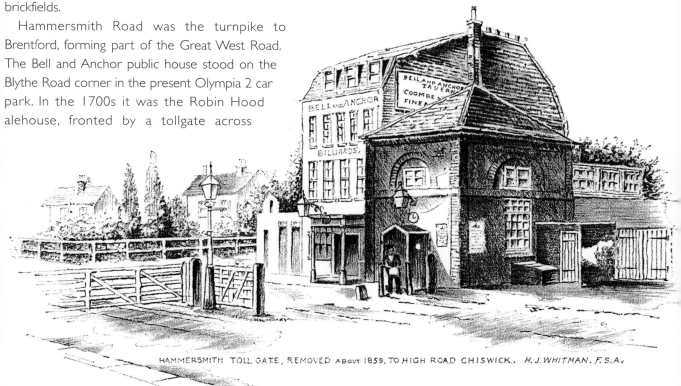

HAMMERSMITH TOLL GATE, REMOVED ABOUT 1859, TO HIGH ROAD CHISWICK.   H.J.WHITMAN. F.S.A.

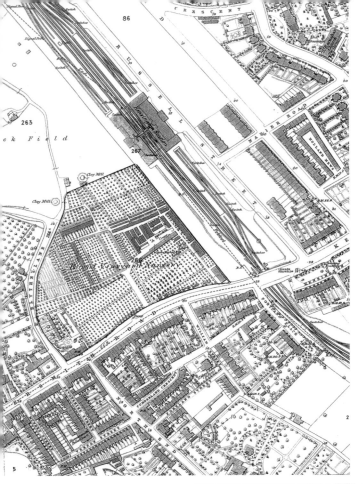

Royal Vineyard Nursery in 1871 where today's Olympia stands. The Bell and Anchor pub is on the Blythe Road corner with a bowling green behind, both now covered by Olympia 2 car park. *(Crown copyright, Ordnance Survey, 1863)*

Olympia, 1896. General manager Gus Harris's ornamental gardens and palm house opened that May on the plot of nearly 6 acres shown beside the hall. It was to be Olympia's land bank for future expansion, now occupied by today's post office on the Blythe Road corner and the big PO building behind it. Note also West Kensington Gardens and the Bell and Anchor pub fronting Hammersmith Road. The former were replaced by the National Hall in 1923 and Empire Hall (now Olympia 2) in 1930. *(Crown copyright, Ordnance Survey, 1896)*

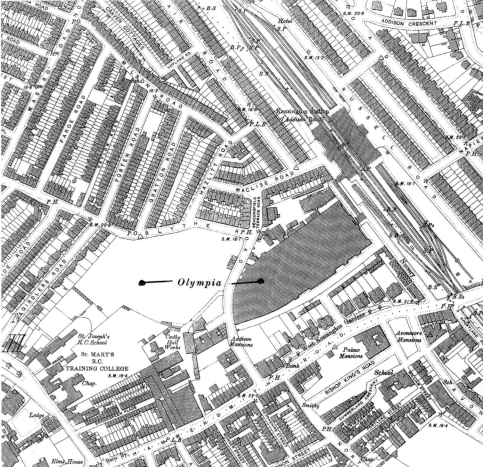

Hammersmith Road. As this relieved thirsty wagoners and carters of their beer money to the detriment of trade, innkeeper John Tunks kept up a long-running feud with the toll collector. When the latter accused Tunks of assault and obstruction the turnpike's trustees successfully opposed renewal of Tunks' liquor licence in 1754. His successor Mark Conture changed the name of the pub, and so it remained until its demolition after the Second World War.

Olympia's site had been a vineyard producing much good Burgundy wine in the mid-eighteenth century. References in the early 1600s to a cottage called 'Vynehouse' and to Henry Bristowe, a wine cooper, suggest it was a vineyard even then. A thatched cottage in the grounds, possibly the Vynehouse, was once occupied by Thomas Worlidge (died 1766), a celebrated artist and engraver who completed some of his best work there. The upper floor was a dwelling-cum-wineshop with wine cellars beneath.

The Vineyard became an internationally celebrated nursery of that name following its purchase by James Lee (1715–95), a gifted Scottish gardener who had left his native Selkirk in about 1732 to walk to London, prudently carrying a sword of Toledo steel made by Andrea Ferrara. He later came under the patronage of the Earl of Islay who was noted for the exotic gardens of his house at Twickenham. Lee was employed there until about the year 1745 when he entered into a partnership with Lewis Kennedy, gardener to Lord Bolton of Chiswick. Lee bought the vineyard, and through their respective patrons he and Kennedy met and mixed freely with botanical scholars and built up a clientele of the nobility. They procured specimens of every new plant as soon as it was introduced by others, and themselves introduced many novelties into the country including oaks from America, ericas, ixias and other Cape plants from South Africa, lobelia from Botany Bay seed, and South American fuchsias which they sold for a guinea a plant. They very profitably introduced the first China rose in 1787. Lewis Kennedy's son John later shipped enormous quantities of plants from the nursery to the Empress Josephine of France, one batch in 1803 costing £2,600. He introduced the standard rose tree into England fifteen years later.

On the deaths of Lee and Kennedy their sons continued the business until 1818 when they dissolved the partnership, the nursery becoming the property of James Lee the younger. It passed on his death in 1827 to his son John who was still there when the National Agricultural Hall Company purchased the site for Olympia. By then it had shrunk to a plants and seeds shop at 2 Hammersmith Road. The reduced parcel of land and greenhouses lay behind, known as the Royal Vineyard Nursery. The rest of the valuable frontage to the road had been sold in 1873 for the construction of the West Kensington Gardens properties.

Having secured the site, the National Agricultural Hall Company commissioned Henry Edward Coe of 4 Furnival's Inn to design the building. With his late partner he had designed the Agricultural Hall at Islington twenty-five years before, and now took its barrel-roof form as the basis for the new building. Its ambitious 170ft clear span would be 40ft wider than the Islington structure. Right round the base of his steeply arched roof he fitted a skirt of pitched roofing to cover a broad gallery that encircled an open well above the arena at ground level. There was fixed seating for 9,000. At

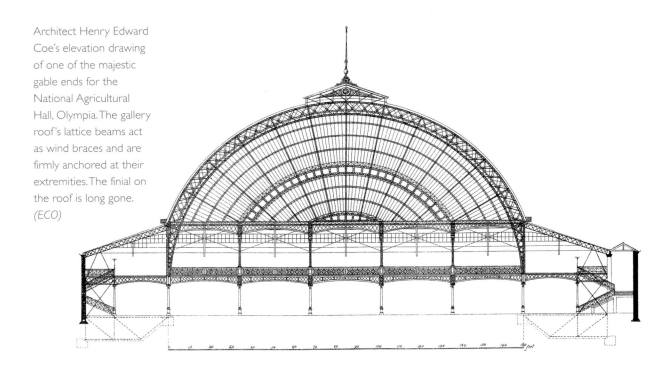

Architect Henry Edward Coe's elevation drawing of one of the majestic gable ends for the National Agricultural Hall, Olympia. The gallery roof's lattice beams act as wind braces and are firmly anchored at their extremities. The finial on the roof is long gone. (ECO)

nearly an acre, the arena was far larger than any other roofed arena in England and probably Europe. Each of the gallery's handsome cast-iron balustrade panels bears a prominent wheatsheaf motif reflecting the hall's original purpose.

Detailed roof design followed from Messrs A.T. Walmisley and M. Am-Ende, engineers of 7 Westminster Chambers. Coe's specification took their expertise close to the limits. The roof had to be high – 115ft at the apex – to enable its great weight to be carried down as near vertically as possible. The loads of the 1,200-ton iron frame plus 85 tons of glass and 75 tons of zinc are most elegantly carried by ten cast-iron columns along either side with a ball and socket bearing at the top and bottom of each to absorb stress. Handyside & Co. of Derby fabricated the ironwork. It was very strong – the hurricane of 1987 achieved no more than the destruction of a loose ventilation hatch.

Lucas & Son of Kensington were to construct the four acres of buildings for £131,573 – today's cost of refurbishing a single toilet suite at Olympia. They had plenty of experience of complex structures, having been involved in the building of the Aggie. The foundation stone was laid by the Earl of Zetland, president of the company, on 21 July 1885. It is tucked away in a corner off the Grand Hall's main entrance.

The roof was erected in twelve weeks in midwinter. Its non-putty patent glazing ensured free expansion and contraction of 2,500-odd sheets of quarter-inch plate glass bedded on zinc-clad timber frames on the weather side, avoiding all painting. This was replaced in 1991 with a sealed heat-treated solar reflective system. Less successful was the infilling of the huge open gable ends. They were fully glazed on steel framing of 'ridge and furrow' construction to give a pleated curtain effect. Unfortunately the corrugation trapped high winds and later one end was partially blown in. They were replaced with the present framework.

Sailors used to heights were engaged for the dangerous job of repainting the gable ends in 1907. Ropes were rigged horizontally across them at intervals, and the seamen spread out along each, one hand on the glazing bar and the other gripping a brush. From a distance they looked like flies caught in a monstrous web, their legs ineffectually flailing. The roof is a marvel of light, balance and strength. It attracted many leading architects and constructors of the day.

Sadly, Coe had to resign through ill-health and died towards the end of 1885. He was succeeded by James Edmeston. Coe's death presumably gave rise to one of Olympia's many legends. It is still said that the designer of the heavy curved 'travellers' which roll along either side of the roof exterior for maintenance purposes, had committed suicide after fellow engineers condemned them as unworkable. But Coe can rest easy; they are still going strong.

A slightly more credible legend surrounds the 'Prince's Apartments', a suite tacked on to the north side of the hall on two floors with rear access from Blythe Road via a small gated yard. It appears on the original building plans under that name. The story goes that the suite was used by Prince Edward for his liaisons – he had a notorious eye for pretty women. The block was rebuilt in 1937 as management offices and meeting rooms, but is still known as the 'Prince's Suite'.

The other building of note was the stunning Minor Hall, long since renamed the Pillar Hall. A sumptuous oak-panelled banqueting room with marble columns and a

The magnificent National Agricultural Hall after its opening in 1886. Addison Road station was renamed Kensington Olympia in 1946. *(ECO)*

richly moulded and decorated ceiling, it is one of London's least known yet most beautiful public rooms.

Stabling with 150 stalls around an open yard filled the 2½ acres between the west end of the main hall and Blythe Road. The east end's neo-classical façade in brick and Portland stone in the Italian style fronts the railway station. A fine frieze above the main entrance was later most unforgivably cut through, possibly in 1955, to make a doorway into what is still known as 'The Dark Room'. Little remains. An original statue of Britannia was certainly removed from over the main entrance in 1955. Its present whereabouts is unknown – someone's garden perhaps?

The hall was lit with nine large suspended lanterns, each containing six electric arc-lamps of enormous candlepower from the Anglo-American Brush Co. A further 1,000 incandescent lamps completed the job. They were powered by Siemens dynamos coupled to two Davey Paxman steam engines in the basement. In 1989 chief rigger Terry Soper discovered fifteen original 2ft diameter glass lamp globes tucked away in a remote corner. A piped hot-water heating system struggled to hold a hall temperature of 56 degrees Fahrenheit (13.5 centigrade) when it was freezing outside. This may not sound very impressive by today's standards but the boiler was trying to warm half a million cubic metres of ambient air – 600 tons – the warmest layer lying under the roof.

Olympia was to become a place of dreams, high endeavour, low cunning, triumphs and occasional tragedies. Above all it was a place of education in the widest sense, and of laughter. In its earliest days M. Jean Franc Gravelet – 'Blondin' – thrilled and terrified audiences with his antics on the high wire; Sankey and Moody held massive revivalist meetings there; and a bullfight, one only, was staged to general disgust.

By 1886 it was clear that the Tournament was not going to leave Islington. Olympia's financial problems worsened but fate dealt it a lucky break. The Paris winter venue of the Hippodrome Circus was closed for repair following a fire, and a London fixture happened to be what the show wanted. The Hippodrome was in a class of its own. It claimed to put more acts and animals into an arena than anyone else in Europe, and to produce the largest and most spectacular performances anywhere. For its London debut at Olympia, 300 horses, 6 'funny' elephants, numerous deer and dogs plus 400

performers and attendants complete with wagon-loads of props, costumes, chariots, animal fodder, cages and tackle streamed out of Addison Road station and into the hall.

Olympia first opened its doors on 26 December 1886. Public transport to get there ranged from a hansom cab (two shillings from a club in Pall Mall, tip optional) to the Metropolitan District Railway, or one of 126 horse-buses that daily passed the end of an extremely muddy Addison Road between the hall and the railway. Recent snow and heavy wagons had turned the unsurfaced road into a morass of mud and gravel, bringing a rebuke in *The Times* next day. Nevertheless, all 9,000 seats were packed with an audience which must have been stunned by the stupendous scale and beauty of the auditorium. The arc-lights high in the shadowed glass vault above them made brilliant the largest indoor arena ever seen in London. A hundred musicians filled the hall with sound. The twenty-eight private boxes fronting the promenade beside the arena had all been snapped up at £2 2s each, likewise the remaining thirty smaller boxes behind them at half the price. If a seat in the stalls at 5s was a bit too steep, there was always

Olympia, c. 1920. National Hall was built on its south (left) flank in 1922 after demolition of houses in West Kensington Gardens and the old Vineyard Nursery buildings visible fronting Addison Road. *(Simmons Aerofilms)*

THE GRAPHIC

AN ILLUSTRATED WEEKLY NEWSPAPER

No. 892.—Vol. XXXV.
Registered as a Newspaper]

SATURDAY, JANUARY 1, 1887

TWO EXTRA
SUPPLEMENTS [

PRICE SIXPENCE
By Post Sixpence Halfpenny

BEATING THE RECORD

RIDING THREE TANDEM AT HURDLES

Olympia's inaugural event, the 'Paris Hippodrome', 1886/7. The chariot racing drove audiences wild. *(GHL, The Graphic)*

GENERAL VIEW OF THE INTERIOR: RIDING THIRTY HORSES BAREBACK

"OLYMPIA," THE NEW PLACE OF ENTERTAINMENT IN KENSINGTON

PERFORMANCES BY THE COMPANY FROM THE PARIS HIPPODROME

the grand circle at half a crown, or standing room in the amphitheatre for a bob. So great were the distances that when Barnum & Bailey's Circus came to Olympia it advised those with weak eyesight to buy Bateman's patent 'Usebius' pince-nez.

Under the masterly direction of M. Houke the show presented a Roman spectacle, feats of horsemanship, sporting events, pantomime and performing animals. Olympia's Mr Wood was sufficiently carried away to claim that additionally a train would appear 'with locomotive, tender and wagons, carrying more than a hundred travellers at express speed!' The dashing post-chaise driving of M. Felix Legay with no fewer than twenty-four high-stepping horses in hand brought gasps of admiration, while the unfamiliar jumping up and down and grappling of a French-style wrestling competition attracted as much laughter as technical appreciation. Two elephants gave a 'concert', one cranking a barrel organ while the other rang bells, having prudently shut the music book first. They rocked on a see-saw when the keeper's back was turned, before gravely taking seats to order dinner. Menus were studied, the waiter finally tipped and the diners ended with a waltz together. As a finale one of the pair rode a bicycle around the arena. The audience was in perpetual fits of laughter.

There followed an interval, during which many male occupants of the stalls and boxes took the opportunity to view the stables and meet the trainers. The ladies could promenade and contemplate the souvenir stalls, among whose offerings were an 'Olympia' perfume called 'the Grecian Esprit', at 1s to 5s 6d a bottle from, somewhat disconcertingly, an Ipswich source. They returned to find the arena transformed into a sylvan scene with hedgerows, cottages, a smithy, mill and stream. Only the juxtaposition of roses in bloom beneath leafless trees jarred. A romantic pantomime involving the miller's daughter and the smith was followed by a highly realistic deer-hunt with French beagles in full cry. The riders were comically represented, from the hapless novice on a weedy screw to the immaculately turned out young miss on a 17-hand hunter.

The outstanding events of the evening were the Roman games. They culminated in truly furious chariot racing between four-abreast teams driven by helmeted heroes in authentic garb. Behind a rising pall of sawdust the huge audience rose to its feet and cheered them on, hats and handkerchiefs waving in a frenzy of encouragement lasting several minutes.

Queen Victoria admires lion cubs at the Hippodrome Circus, Olympia, 19 March 1887. *(ECO)*

In this her Golden Jubilee year, Queen Victoria attended a private Saturday morning performance on 19 March 1887 with the children of the Duke of Connaught, Prince Henry of Battenburg and Princess Beatrice, and a small entourage. They were received by the Earl of Lathom and M. Houcke before taking their seats on a hastily constructed dais in the otherwise empty hall. Victoria had not attended a public entertainment in years and no thought had been given to provision of a royal box. The party watched an abbreviated one-hour show, the Queen laughing and clapping with the others at the performing elephants and the chariot racers. They later toured the stables, fed the elephants and handled a lion cub. Long denied the opportunity to see their queen, the public was pleased to view the flower-bedecked dais which remained in situ for the afternoon and evening performances.

After her years of self-imposed isolation the Queen's sudden reappearance in public, and at a 'foreign' production, was resented by some of the English theatrical community. Their suspicion that she favoured imported productions over the home-grown variety was reinforced in May by the two Royal Command performances given by the Wild West Show. It was more than some old stagers could bear. Vesta Tilley, the darling of the music halls, gave vent in song:

> She's seen the Yankee buffaloes,
> the circus too from France,
> and may she reign until she gives
> the English show a chance.

> *chorus*

> May Queen Victoria reign,
> may she long with us remain,
> 'til Irving* takes rank with a war-painted Yank,
> may good Queen Victoria reign.

While the two newcomers to London's entertainment scene that year presented giant shows on an unparalleled scale, the Agricultural Hall in Islington responded with the enchanting 'Arcadia', a pantomime in a fairyland setting. Its centrepiece was a monster waterfall 45ft high and as much across, illuminated by limelights in the dimmed auditorium. The cast had to shout every line to be heard above the noise of 120,000 gallons per hour crashing down behind them.

At Olympia the National Agricultural Hall Company was in financial difficulty. It had been close to insolvency when the Hippodrome Circus began delivering attendances which exceeded 369,000 in the first eight weeks alone. Public response to the shares issue had been disappointing. Take-up was not helped by the looming threat of competition from Earls Court – rivalry between the two centres would run on for another eighty-six years. As a sweetener, buyers of twenty-five or more Olympia shares

* Sir Henry Irving was king of the English stage.

were offered life membership with free admission to the hall and gardens whenever they were open to the public. A further incentive to reach for cheque books was the Earl of Zetland's appointment of some two hundred vice-presidents. His parliamentary connections doubtless secured the eighty peers and sixty knights among them.

Other attempts to generate cash included a Carriage Department supervised by coachmaker Mr J.W. Turner which offered showroom and sale facilities for 'high class carriages, especially patents and those of newest design'. A display gallery for them was strategically sited between the two tiers of private boxes overlooking the arena. The surplus phaetons, landaus and broughams of the gentry were charged at 3s per week for display, and 5 per cent of the value of any sale.

The Hippodrome Circus had been followed in 1887 by a Sportsman's Exhibition, an Exhibition of Sporting Dogs by Mr Charles Cruft, a national gymnastic meeting with over 2,000 competitors, and a horse show. October brought the return of the Hippodrome Circus. Colonel Cody's triumphant Wild West Show down the road was now packing its bags and selling off its horses before embarking for home, while the resourceful M. Houcke had brought over a French version based on the colonisation of Algeria. Arabs replaced Red Indians and the French army took over from the cowboys. A neat piece of theatre brought the soldiers into the arena aboard an armoured train which puffed and screeched right round the circuit on a Decauville light railway system installed during the interval. Other highlights included Miss Jenny O'Brien's hair-raising ride standing upright on a horse at full gallop while – wait for it – driving a thundering team of thirty-two horses ahead of her. Chariot racing was further enlivened with eight-horse teams in place of four. Steeple-chasing required riders to stand astride two jumpers while controlling another pair ahead – almost beyond belief. Each year the limit of human (and equine) achievement seemed to go up another notch.

The Irish Exhibition in 1888 was the first of Olympia's set-piece re-creations, featuring aspects of Irish life, work and industry. A stone-built and Donegal-thatched village lay outside in the gardens, each cottage demonstrating some handicraft. It was joined by a substantial castle and tower. Blarney Castle complete with a replica Blarney stone was the inevitable goal for many on arrival.

The National Agricultural Hall Company had managed to clear its debts and fend off a winding-up petition in January 1888 before seeking fresh capital once more. It slid into receivership twelve months later, barely two years after first opening its doors. The Hippodrome had twice delivered a cash bonanza but Olympia struggled for too much of the intervening time. The company was put in the hands of liquidator Thomas Welton who kept the business going in hopes of finding a buyer. Lettings that year were again thin but included the First Great Horse Show, a Kennel Club dog show and, rather oddly, a Rejected Royal Academy Picture Exhibition. However, a circus returned to Olympia for the 1889–90 season with Phineas T. Barnum's 'Greatest Show on Earth'.

Old Barnum was to circus what Cody was to cowboys. The showman brought his gigantic production over from New York and squeezed into the Olympia hall not one but three rings, separated by two stages for speciality acts and acrobats. All five were in furious action, the effect being kaleidoscopic as it was impossible to follow every performance at once. Barnum well knew this, his philosophy being to throw the entire repertoire into a single heap and let the audience sort out its own delights. Then the tempo changed, and the many acts gave way to a single historical spectacle, always on the largest scale.

For the Olympia feature Barnum had approached Imre Kiralfy, a 44-year-old Hungarian émigré who had recently produced in New York a wildly ambitious creation of Nero's Burning of Rome. His 1,500 performers were on a stage nearly 500ft wide, cued via a line of electric bells set in the stage front. One scene change brought 500 cast members into view clinging to a mountainside, the huge set rotating into position on rails. Barnum wanted the show for Olympia. So, it turned out, did Kiralfy. With some scaling down and much chariot racing, 'The Destruction of Rome' took London by storm.

Receiver Tom Welton changed tack after Barnum's departure. Three or four spot lettings for brief events between April and October were hardly going to transform the business. He collaborated with an American roller-skating promoter and £6,000 was invested in decking over the entire asphalt ground floor between the galleries with 1½ acres of beech and maple board. They hoped to revive a flagging craze for 'rinking'. Until then, skate wheels wore out after a few hours. Olympia's rink was stocked with 10,000 pairs of skates with the new hemacite-coated wheels on ball bearings which

transformed the hobby. The glassy, beautifully mitred surface opened in April 1890 to a hearty public welcome, the band of the Honourable Artillery Company and stunt demonstrations.

Fifty tactful instructors in peaked caps and braided lion-tamer tunics were on hand daily to tend the fallen. During the last few minutes of each session 'fast skating' was permitted, novices hastily removing themselves from the speeding traffic. The management announced 'a future series of entertainments from which every objectionable feature will be rigidly excluded, and in which gentlemen and ladies young and old may participate with pleasure and advantage as a most salutary athletic exercise'. Fancy dress carnivals typified these events. The first prize of £100 in one such competition went to skater James Tatem as 'Electricity' – he was festooned with batteries, telephones, coils and 'phonographs'. Runner-up Bruce Smith as 'Hymen Up to Date' wore a heart on his breast, slippers on his shoulders, a bride's veil and a wedding cake on his head.

The hobby was so widely accepted that 'do you rink' became a young man's opening gambit. One of Du Maurier's cartoons had a lisping youth in immaculate top hat and frock coat asking a primly 'correct' young miss:

Do you evah wink, Miss Evangeline?
Do I ever *what*, Mr Smythe?
Wink?
What *do* you mean, sir?
Well, skate if you pwefer the expwession?

Olympia's rink closed in September the following year to make room for undoubtedly the most ambitious 'spectacular' ever to be staged inside and outside the hall.

It came about this way. The concession for Olympia's food and drink sales had been newly won by Joseph 'Joe' Lyons, soon to become Britain's king of mass catering. Lyons was fired with ambition to stage a spectacular of his own, filling the hall and the 5½ acres of gardens around it. He discussed possibilities with his dynamic friend Harold Hartley, mineral water supplier and chairman of the Pure Water Company. Their ideas ranged from old London to the Orient, water being a key ingredient. Hartley later claimed that it was Lyons who finally suggested Venice, and 'Venice in London' it became. They secured an option on Olympia for a full year's occupation. Rent would be payable from the show's opening day at £300 per week. The period to build it was rent-free. They raised £18,000 and cabled Imre Kiralfy in America: 'Will you come over and produce Venice in London at Olympia and if so on what terms?' He replied simply: 'I am leaving by next boat.'

Kiralfy asserts that the Venice idea was his, flashing across his mind while he was at Barnum's Connecticut home. In any case terms were agreed and a syndicate called Imre Kiralfy Ltd was formed (although Kiralfy himself held no personal interest in it). He took a ground-floor flat in Addison Court Gardens and went on to design and stage at unprecedented cost a sumptuous re-creation of Venice complete with streets of ancient houses, cafés, shops full of tempting curios and displays of lace-making and

Venetian glass-blowing, plentiful canals, a hundred Venetian Gondoliers and thirty imported gondolas. These last had to be specially made as the standard craft were found on arrival to be 8ft too long for the Olympia layout.

The hall was divided longitudinally into three broad strips. On the left was an enormous stage almost the full length of the building; down the centre was a vast lake fronting the stage; and behind the lake was the seating for 8,000. The canal network led from the lake out of the hall and into the gardens and the buildings of Venice. The lake and canals were to be lined with concrete, but dismantling costs prohibited this and lead had to be used – many tons of impossibly expensive lead sheet. The problem threatened not so much to blow the show out of the water, as the water out of the show. Montagu Gluckstein, a director of Imre Kiralfy Ltd and reckoned by Hartley to be one of the most astute businessmen he had ever met, suggested hiring the lead instead. Hartley soon found a willing supplier.

Hartley's admiration for Gluckstein's acumen was well justified. He was once invited to Buzzards, a famous cake shop in Oxford Street which was a customer of his, to see the firm's new catering venture. Montagu Gluckstein also had interests in the food business as a director of J. Lyons & Co., so the two went together. Buzzards had opened an afternoon tea department. Gluckstein said at once: 'This must be our next game.' Lyons went into retail catering and its teashops sprang up everywhere, followed by the famous Lyons Corner Houses. Joe Lyons' fortune – and a national institution – was born at Buzzards.

The Venetian extravaganza opened on Boxing Day 1891. It ran for thirteen months and cost £60,000 – a sum which was recovered in the first three months. The twice-daily performances were phenomenal. Each ended with a grand ballet of a thousand dancers. The *Daily Graphic* set the scene:

First, there are the brightly lighted stalls where damsels, Venetian in costume if not in accent, coax the visitor to lay out his spare cash on fans, flowers, trinkets or sweets. Refreshment bars and little tête à tête tables are scattered about where visitors can sit to watch the passing throng, while big burly Venetian Gendarmes lounge about, endeavouring in their best English to direct enquirers to distant parts of Venice, and little boys in uniform, armed with toy dirks, are dealing out programmes and views of the exhibition.

Passing through the bazaar at the back of the great hall where the grand ballet takes place, by heaps of furniture, statuary, pianos and some very fine hammered brass and ironwork, the visitor comes to the gate of modern Venice. Over the parapet of the first bridge a crowd of curious sightseers hang to watch the gondolas dodge under the arch. Beyond them is Venice proper, with its little shops full of tempting curiosities, its quaint buildings, arcades and canal-side corners where every moment a gondola glides past in its 'tour round the town'. Further

Imre Kiralfy, King of Spectacle. (Exhibition Study Group: Strand Magazine, 1909)

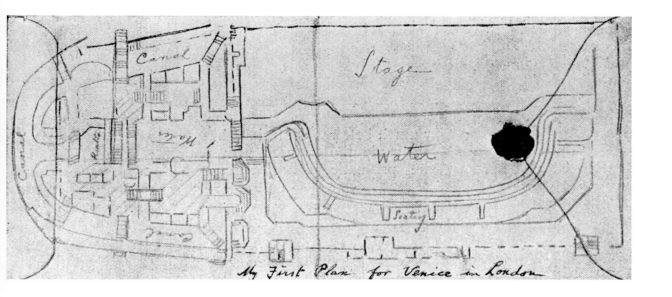

My First Plan for Venice in London

down the canal but within hearing of the café, the gondola singers are amusing a large audience on the Grand Canal with Venetian songs and dances, accompanying themselves on the mandolin, guitar and violin. The comedian of the company is a tremendously funny fellow, and the English listeners, though few of them probably understand a word of the song, cheer and encore with great spirit. In another part of Venice a balcony concert attracts a large number of people and forms a very pretty sight.

At half past eight the City is all but deserted, for then the Grand Ballet begins – in which all the thousand dancers are attired in gorgeous costumes elaborately and carefully finished. . . . Towards the end a line of dancers, extending from one end of Olympia to the other, dance down the stage towards the water in perfect time, making up one of the most spectacular effects ever seen in London.

Debt-laden Olympia was sold at auction by the Official Receiver in February 1893. It went for £140,000 to the Freehold Syndicate, an unregistered vehicle formed in January solely to purchase the venue and to sell it on at a profit. The syndicate's trustees were the entire board of Imre Kiralfy Ltd: Lyons, Hartley, Gluckstein and secretary John Hart. They were well placed to put a value on Olympia's assets and prospects, and days later the syndicate sold the business for £180,000, taking a net profit of £34,000. The purchaser was Olympia Ltd, a company which at that point did not exist but which the four promoted and proceeded to register in March with nominal capital of £225,000 in shares and debentures. Unsurprisingly, Lyons, Hartley, Gluckstein and Herman Hart (John's brother) joined the board. Olympia Ltd was bound by the conditions of sale to award the catering contract to J. Lyons & Co. and to appoint J. & H. Hart as its advertising agents.

The vast cost and scale of the Venetian canals and buildings made it essential that these assets were retained for a second season. But as what? The new company decided on an Oriental production based on Constantinople. Imre Kiralfy's expensive

The Hall of the Thousand and One Pillars at Kiralfy's 'Constantinople', Olympia, 1893–4. Mirrors and dim lighting enhanced the subterranean effect. (GHL, The Graphic)

agreement having expired, his brother Bolossy was engaged to produce the show on less demanding terms. His 'Constantinople, or the Revels of the East' opened on Boxing Day 1893 as a 'Grand Terpsichorean, Romantic and Lyric Spectacle and Aquatic Pageant in Two Acts and Six Tableaux'. Glittering golden-domed buildings and bazaars replaced Venice, and caiques manned by Arab boatmen took visitors on trips culminating in a slow passage through the Hall of the Thousand and One Pillars. This much-remarked moonlit marvel of mirrors and plasterwork presented an authentic likeness of the ancient Cistern of Constantine, an underground lake beneath the city. The mirrors gave an endless perspective of Byzantine columns and lapping water in cavernous gloom.

Bolossy shrewdly brought the show right to the railway station's entrance. Arriving visitors instantly found themselves in an enclosed vaulted 'street' of pillars and arches with a mix of Oriental shops and modern advertising posters.

A serious diplomatic incident arose when Turkish government representatives visited the show and were confronted with a set-piece Turkish harem whose ladies made great sport of their lord and master, the Sultan. They insisted on its immediate withdrawal. Grovelling apologies were made to the Turkish Ambassador, who was persuaded to see the show from the royal box. Determined to shoot themselves in both feet, the management left in a very realistic scene of a slave market – which further enraged the ambassador until Joe Lyons assured him that slaves were sold openly on the streets of London. Though less popular than 'Venice', the show with its 2,000 performers ran for nearly two years until November 1894 and was judged by *The Times* to have exceeded its predecessor in creativity and entertainment. More than 32,000 people attended the opening day.

In 1892 Joe Lyons' headquarters had been an Olympia basement room with one telephone and one typewriter. Two years later in August 1894 he moved into Cadby Hall, his newly built food factory in Blythe Road opposite Olympia.

The hall staged yet another variant on 'Venice' for the winter season, which was already almost upon them. 'The Orient' opened on the now traditional Boxing Day in 1894, barely a month after 'Constantinople' had closed. Bolossy, whose background was the theatre, had gone one better than his brother's balletic finale in which the line of 1,000 performers danced to the water's edge. He advanced them across the water on an extending stage. This novelty allowed two lines of dancers to trip out in pairs on to each of two great catwalk arcs which slowly emerged from either end of the main stage, to glide out across the water and join as a half-circle of one thousand dancers in the centre of the lake. The hundreds remaining on the fixed stage formed the other half of what became a giant ring of colour and movement, the wonderfully lit 'Circular Ballet' bringing the house down.

Although over 34,000 attended on the opening day, breaking all records, numbers fell away during three months of severe frosts and a subsequent influenza epidemic. Low revenues forced the show's closure in July 1895. It also propelled Olympia Ltd

In Olympia's gallery, preparing wall and ceiling panels for 'Constantinople', 1893. *(ECO)*

'The Orient' at Olympia, 1894/5. A thousand dancers perform on two giant platforms as they glide out from the stage over water to join and form a half-circle. Bolossy Kiralfy was a master of theatrical effects. (GHL, The Graphic)

into liquidation. The principal creditors, Allsopps Breweries, foreclosed on a mortgage of £17,500 and secured a winding-up order. The huge costs of 'The Orient' included £20,000 for costumes alone. The creditors proposed the formation of a new company under the same name to acquire the assets and liabilities of the old. It would be capitalised at £225,000 in £1 shares, the old business and its debts to be secured in return for shares. The second Olympia Ltd was accordingly formed in August for this purpose. Montagu Gluckstein and his three associates were not invited to join the board.

Gluckstein was later summonsed by the liquidator of the original Olympia Ltd and charged with breach of trust in that he, Lyons, Hartley and Herman Hart as directors of the company had secretly obtained £6,341 and allegedly divided it between themselves, this being part of the purchase money paid by the company to acquire Olympia in 1893. The summons was dismissed, but upheld on appeal by the Official Receiver.

FOUR
OLYMPIA
New Direction

'The first sight of Olympia outside at night is strikingly weird and fantastic. The huge roof through which the rays of light inside faintly penetrate, and the two great electric lamps pendant over the central entrance [while] inside all is brilliancy and sparkle.'

Daily Graphic, 22 March 1892

OLYMPIA HAD THREE OWNERS in its first ten years and the hall was in liquidation or receivership for all but the first two. Now, in August 1895, its creditors were on the bridge, concerned only to steer the second Olympia Ltd at speed into profitable waters before jumping ship with their dues. Sir Augustus 'Gus' Harris, the 43-year-old king of London theatre, joined the board as a major shareholder. He was revered and feared by all. Superhuman energy drove him to run simultaneously the capital's two great royal theatres and six or seven other playhouses, numerous tours and imported attractions. General manager Wallace Jones was given little time and less funding with which to put together Olympia's winter programme. It was too late anyway to book the big shows. Undeterred, Harris accepted the challenge, marrying a dramatic re-creation of the Siege of Chitral (which noisily consumed much black powder), with a string of cycling tournaments. This unlikely pairing ran successfully for seven months.

The following February Lady Harris, Gus's wife, attended Robert Paul's demonstration of his 'Theatrograph' (cine projector) before members of the Royal Institution. It was only the second demonstration of motion pictures to be given before a scientific body in Great Britain. Paul was summoned to join Gus Harris for breakfast next morning, 1 March 1896. A deal was struck – Paul would screen his moving pictures at Olympia forthwith. He and Gus treated this historic occasion as no more than a diversion, though it was one of the very first picture shows London ever saw. The public flocked to see the flickering images of the 'Animatograph', as Paul renamed his apparatus. He almost certainly screened 'A Shoeblack at Work in a London Street' and 'A Rough Sea at Dover', the films which he had presented to the Royal Institution only days before. There was an early cinema in the ballroom-sized area above Olympia's Pillar Hall. It has been a staff restaurant for many years, but a projectionist's window remains high up in an end wall. However, Paul's screenings very probably pre-date this.

Gus Harris was in the same league as Bolossy Kiralfy. He was happiest when marshalling casts of hundreds, even thousands, and creating technically brilliant events on stage – the Grand National with real horses over jumps; a sinking troopship; a train crash. He could not even stage the pantomime 'The Forty Thieves' without boosting their numbers to four hundred, ignoring the entreaties of his backers.

The first Olympia Ltd had purchased the freehold of nearly 6 acres of open ground on the other side of Blythe Road as a land bank. The new owners turned it into pleasure gardens that spring. These were approached from the north-west corner of the main building via a broad ramped subway beneath Blythe Road, brilliantly lit and resplendent with mirrors and murals. Emerging at the far end one entered a great palm house. Its 40ft-high roof was supported by pillars disguised as palm trees, with the real thing in profusion. The façade and side of the building totalled nearly 500ft according to the *West London Observer*, which suggests a covered area approaching an acre. It was to double as a permanent sub-tropical garden and a refuge for first-class concerts and other entertainment in wet weather. Elegant terraces across the frontage provided for al fresco dinners, teas and smoking promenades. In the grounds a central bandstand nestled among densely planted borders and shrubberies and lofty surrounding trees. A grand panorama of the Bay of Naples and Vesuvius ran along the south boundary, beside which were extensive shooting ranges with picturesque scenery and realistic game for the shooters. Beyond that again in the south-west corner was an open-air variety theatre. The whole area was awash with gas lighting in discreetly coloured globes.

Only weeks after London's great and good thronged the opening of the gardens in May 1896, the second Olympia company went into liquidation. The garden site which had cost £18,800 to develop was later sold by Allsopps Breweries, which had taken possession of Olympia after paying out the other debenture holders. Today's post office and the monolithic PO Savings Bank behind it were built on the garden grounds in 1899.

Olympia's stables were replaced by a glass-roofed Winter Garden as a lower extension off the end of the main hall. It was a more practical revenue-earner which retained some of the atmosphere of the short-lived garden venture across the road. This annexe remains in service as exhibition space.

Sadly, Sir Augustus Harris died of a wasting disease and overwork on 22 June. The eagle had burned out in mid-flight. Allsopps appointed one of its directors, Frederick Harold Payne, as managing director of the Olympia operation. 'Pa' Payne's immediate problem was to find a tenancy for the year end with only weeks to go. In some desperation he put together a Christmas show for the few motorists then about, and the idly curious. The first motor show to be staged in Britain had taken place only the previous year, 1895, at the Tunbridge Wells home of David Salomons, founder-member of the Self-Propelled Traffic Association which had been campaigning against the restrictive Highways Acts. Five automobiles were exhibited at the unassuming one-day event in his garden. He had lit the touch-paper – others rode the rocket.

Olympia's International Motor Show and Cycle Tournament opened over Christmas 1896. It was a necessary marriage of machines because the few available cars would barely have filled the foyer. Motor shows had been held earlier that year at Crystal Palace and the Imperial Institute, the larger Palace event displaying some twenty

vehicles. The Aggie staged one with the publishers of *The Motor Car Journal*, and this event became an annual fixture. Olympia's timing, however, was perfect: the 'Red Flag Act' was abolished days before the show opened and automobiles could now proceed without a flagman walking ahead. As the fastest recorded speed that year was 10mph there was little chance of anyone actually getting knocked down. (Only three years later the record reached 70mph.) Payne repeated the experiment in 1897, then abandoned it. Only the wealthy could afford the devilish machines and they were incompatible with carriage horses. Even the Prince of Wales chose not to ride in a motor car until 1898.

Frederick 'Pa' Payne, managing director of
Olympia, 1896–1912. (ECO)

Sporting promoter Ned Cleary turned his hand to an ambitious presentation of life in South Africa for an Olympia season in 1899/1900. Promoters in those days had no hesitation in uprooting simple natives wherever they found them and shipping them over for public display. Many of Buffalo Bill's Indians were prisoners from the Indian wars, released on licence to him by the US government. Cleary's 'Briton, Boer and Black in Savage South Africa' displayed Zulu tribespeople as curiosities, bringing complaints from the public and a rebuke from the local licensing authority.

On the motoring front in 1903 the capital was treated to three shows – at the Aggie, at Paxton's Crystal Palace, the giant glasshouse having moved from Hyde Park to Sydenham Hill after the Great Exhibition, and at Earls Court's showground for the Stanley Automobile Exhibition. This last was a newcomer, taking its name from the Stanley Cycle Club. Its exhibitors included the Lancashire Steam Motor Co. – later Leyland Motors Ltd – which built steam wagons and even steam-powered lawnmowers. The successful Crystal Palace show was the first to be staged by the newly formed Society of Motor Manufacturers and Traders (SMMT). It took 8,000 sq. metres of hall space for 180 exhibitors, jumping to 12,000 sq. metres and 270 stands the following year.

Payne waited no longer. Olympia had to break out of its crippling yearly cycle of feast and famine – the occasional mammoth spectacular punctuated by a handful of generally unproductive dog shows, athletics meetings and the like. National prosperity, and especially the rapidly expanding middle class with its increasing disposable income, was generating an unprecedented demand for goods and services. Producers were quick to respond but lacked the industrial equivalent of the farmers' market. Payne was not entirely alone in foreseeing the coming tide of specialist trade exhibitions, but he was arguably the first in Britain to meet it. He determined to build an annual calendar with a core of solidly reliable trade shows to underpin the business. The capture of the motor show would encourage others to follow.

First, the hall's inflexible installations for arena-based seated events had to go. Space and time remain the hall-owner's key marketable assets and Payne needed all the floor space he could get. There was no year-end show in 1904. Instead the arena and 4,000 permanent tiered seats were ripped out, a new cement floor was laid and lightweight portable seating purchased. At £8,000 it was a costly operation, but having literally cleared the deck Payne netted a clutch of trade and mixed exhibitions and big arena shows over the next five years. Some of them became established 'bankers' and a few are still going strong today.

A dramatic wrestling match was the first event to use the new seating. Its promoter Charles 'Cockie' Cochran (1872–1951) was another great showman of the day. He had cut his theatrical teeth in America after a failed attempt to become an actor at home in England. His management skills soon surfaced and having staged his first production in New York he returned to set up shop in Chancery Lane as a theatrical agent. Cockie

Georges Hackenschmidt, 'The Russian Lion', vs Madrali, 'The Terrible Turk', Olympia, 1904. *(ECO)*

soon had Harry Houdini the escapologist, Mistinguette and various other leading lights on his books. He discovered Georges Hackenschmidt, a giant Russian wrestler, whom he matched against Madrali 'The Terrible Turk.' Skilful promotion had all England speculating on the outcome of the match for which Cochran had booked Olympia – no other venue matched its capacity.

The men met in the ring on 30 January 1904. All the professional punters' money was on the Turk. A fashionable and feverish crowd packed Olympia. The nation waited. Sporting correspondents crouched on the edges of aisle seats, poised to write or run for a cab, as the action dictated. At the bell Hackenschmidt, who had exhibited extreme nervousness in the dressing room, came out like a tiger at the slowly advancing Madrali. Grasping the big Turk around the waist with both arms the Russian lifted him shoulder high before hurling him to the floor with a thud that was heard throughout the hall. Silence turned to shock. It was all over in just 45 seconds. Hackenschmidt had dislocated Madrali's shoulder. Several late arrivals saw nothing for the £5 5s price of their ringside seats. Hackenschmidt became a national hero overnight and took the winner's £1,000 purse, Madrali getting £500. Cochran always claimed afterwards that the Turk had broken both arms, but he was a born huckster and it made a good story better.

Hard choices at the Motor Show, Olympia, 1905. *(GHL, The Graphic)*

The two wrestlers met for a second time in May 1906, again at Olympia, for a stake of £200 plus a percentage of the profits and the world championship. The application of the dreaded 'Madrali grip' for over two minutes in the second bout must have galvanised the Russian, who suddenly turned it to his advantage by rolling Madrali on to his back in a victorious pin-fall, to the indescribable enthusiasm of the audience.

In 1911 Cochran put on his first boxing match at Olympia. The fight was of no great moment; it was more a test of official and public reaction. Pa Payne was warned by the local authority that he was risking Olympia's annual operating licence if the fight went ahead. Cochran did his utmost to persuade the public that his contests were above board and responsibly controlled. He even had a clergyman in full clerical rig to announce the bouts. During the first match a spectator jumped into the ring to protest at such a brutal exhibition in a public place. This did not sufficiently impress the authorities, who allowed boxing to become a regular feature at Olympia.

Olympia's transformation

Payne had little difficulty in persuading the SMMT to bring him its bulging Motor Show. Within two years Olympia's low-rent events had almost vanished, to be replaced by a growing programme of trade and public exhibitions. Olympia's far-reaching change of direction contrasted with that of its rival Earls Court where mammoth months-long shows continued.

The fourth Motor Show arrived at Olympia in February 1905. It was heavily promoted and heavily oversubscribed but astute work secured a repeat show in November. An orchestra played its way along Hammersmith Road with a special composition entitled '*La Belle Chauffeuse*'. Trial runs followed along the road to introduce the public to the joys of motoring. Some cars were brought from the showroom to the hall on the backs of horse-drawn wagons to avoid dirt and road damage. Heavy commercial vehicles, motor-buses, powerboats and motorbikes were included in the show that year, though perhaps not the 'New Wind Motor Cycle' – actually a pushbike fitted with a small windmill up front, shaft-driven from the pedal crank. It was claimed to be ideal in a headwind, the makers quoting extracts from testimonials as proof.

The 4th SMMT Motor Show, Olympia, November 1905. A chain-drive Sunbeam 16–20hp was yours for £530. *(ECO)*

The Aero and Motor Boat Exhibition, Olympia, 1911. Note Louis Bleriot's aeroplanes in the foreground. *(ECO)*

The hall changed hands yet again between the two 1905 Motor Shows. The New Olympia Company Ltd was hardly over-endowed. At £90,000 its capitalisation was equivalent to the cost of staging one Kiralfy production. Payne continued as managing director.

An Arrol-Johnston motorbike was the star of the November show, having won the Isle of Man Tourist Trophy race. There was much amusement on the Argyll stand where a Scottish gentleman had repeatedly pressed them to confirm their claims for a new carburettor. It transpired that he was about to buy a Whites steam car and was contemplating fitting Argyll's carb to improve its fuel economy! One has to remember just how new and unfamiliar the technology was. The War Office prohibited petrol engines for its motor transport, fearing the fire hazard in fuel storage and movement. The first lorries purchased by the Army in 1903 were paraffin (kerosene) oil fuelled, and the petrol embargo ran on for several years.

The SMMT was determined to ensure that it owned and controlled the dominant shop window for the motor industry. Founder members produced an 'Exhibition Covenant' through which they undertook to exhibit only at SMMT shows. The society had insisted as a condition of coming to Olympia that no other tenant would be permitted to display motorised transport of any kind without its consent. By 1906 its original membership of 32 had grown to 400. (In that year 32,451 private cars were on Britain's roads, and an astonishing 12,398 taxis.) The Olympia Motor Show rapidly became (and remained) a hugely popular pre-Christmas fixture, interrupted only by the First World War. It moved to Earls Court in 1937.

The makers of any form of transport fitted with an internal combustion engine became fair game for the SMMT. The net even extended to boats and aeroplanes. The society lumped together commercial vehicles with motor-boats at Olympia in 1907 for the first International Commercial Motor Vehicle and Boat Exhibition. Boats lay next to omnibuses in a maddening mix of the unmatchable. The boats were omitted the following year, and in 1909 the show was cancelled at a late stage for want of commercial vehicle support despite the unpromising inclusion of a few aeroplanes. As rent was still payable for the empty hall the society hastily sought a 'filler'. It put together another unlikely pairing in the Aero and Motor Boat Exhibition, bravely giving space free to all exhibitors to ensure take-up and in the hope of profitable repeat events. The show opened in March 1909 to protests in aviation circles that March was the windiest and therefore most dangerous month for exhibitors to lay on supporting demonstrations in the air. Aeroplanes crashed on a regular basis, often with fatal results. To build a machine that could fly a mile or two was still a considerable achievement. The Aero and Motor Boat Exhibition lost £3,000 but returned to Olympia for two more years. The Commercial Motor Show returned in 1913 before war intervened.

Colonel Cody's last stand at Olympia

Buffalo Bill Cody's 'Wild West' in 1902/3 proved to be the last of Olympia's long-running spectaculars. The colonel had returned to a subdued London that December at the start of his third European tour. The past three years were filled with sombre events and national anxieties for Britain. The country had been at war with the Boers in South Africa since 1899, both sides taking terrible losses. Peace came only in May 1902. Queen Victoria had died and her son Edward, Prince of Wales, had taken the throne in August 1901.

A tense moment for Buffalo Bill in Olympia's arena, 1903. Audiences could buy their children a small box of stand-up cardboard figures of Bill, cowboys and Indians for 1s 6d. (Denver Public Library)

Football on a bouncy 5,900 sq. metres carpet of green raffia 'grass' at Olympia's Winter Palace of Sport, 1905/6. A folding ladder hangs from the roof for the gymnastics. (*GHL, The Graphic*)

On Boxing Day afternoon, as Cody's large company awaited the start of the first performance of a fourteen-week season, the Colonel was devastated to receive a telegram informing him that his close friend and business partner Nate Salsbury had died. Cody wanted to cancel the performance but was persuaded to see it through for the sake of the thousands already taking their seats. The show opened with the many flags around the arena at half-mast. Cody and his performers went through their routines as the professionals they all were, and the audience cheered them to the echo.

King Edward VII and Queen Alexandra attended later, appreciative and gracious as ever. Afterwards they sent Colonel Cody a pin in the form of a crown set with diamonds and rubies. An embarrassing oversight that had marred their arrival at Olympia in 1899 was not repeated. On that occasion they had been attending Lady Randolph Churchill's charity benefit in support of hospital ships during the South African War. As the couple entered the royal box the possibly overwrought bandmaster forgot to strike up the national anthem. Literally rising to the occasion, the audience gave *four* hearty cheers in lieu.

Attendances fell off as the weeks passed, but never the brilliance of the show. In April the entire operation – performers, animals, portable seating and structures, bags and baggage – filled three fifty-carriage show trains at Addison Road station and headed north to Manchester.

The trumpets shall sound

Pa Payne found a promoter to put on a Winter Palace of Sport for the Christmas show of 1905/6. It was notable for its 'grass' carpet, but for little else. The 1½ acre sea of green raffia woven into a coconut fibre backing was made to special order by Harrods, which employed 200 Suffolk weavers for four months to do the job. When trimmed and watered to help it settle, the turf substitute looked the real thing at night from any seat in the house. Unfortunately it proved impossible to persuade any of the football league clubs to play on the bouncy carpet and the whole show was a fiasco. A team of Basque Pelota players was brought over and courts built at great expense for the fastest ball game in the world, but it failed to catch the imagination of the Londoners.

Cochran next stepped in with an idea for a traditional fun-fair and circus. Payne approved, and Cockie's highly successful Mammoth Fun City series of shows filled the Christmas and New Year slot for the next five years. Roller-skating was included from 1907/8 and the craze was reborn – again.

Payne's second victory was the capture of the Royal Naval and Military Tournament which came across from Islington's Royal Agricultural Hall in 1906. It was a matchless blend of entertainment and, less fashionable now, national pride. On 11 June 1880 a notice had appeared in *The Times*:

Artillery crosses a pontoon bridge, an armoured train beyond, at the Royal Military Tournament. *(ECO)*

> A Military Tournament and Assault-At-Arms is to be held from 21st to 26th inst. at the Agricultural Hall, Islington. The Competitions, which are 53 in number, are to be open to all the regiments within range, and the profits are to be given in aid of the funds of the Royal Cambridge Asylum for Soldiers' Widows. They include tilting at the ring, sword v. bayonet, lemon cutting, etc. This is the first time that a general tournament of this kind has been organised. Among the Patrons are the Prince of Wales, the Duke of Connaught, the Duke of Cambridge and Prince Edward of Saxe-Weimar. Major-General E.S. Burnaby MP is the Hon. Sec.

The idea almost certainly sprang from the annual summer meetings of the National Rifle Association on Wimbledon Common where the crack shots of the volunteer regiments slugged it out. In the long intervals they made up informal sporting competitions of a military character, and so the thing developed. Its charitable purpose contributed hugely to the Royal Cambridge Asylum for Soldiers' Widows, the Duke of Cambridge memorably expressing the hope 'that every Regiment in the Army will soon have a widow in the Institution'.

The first tournaments were concerned solely with skill at arms and horsemanship. The Navy joined in 1905, and in 1906 the event was dominated by demonstrations of skirmishing in bush and desert, a historical pageant, a musical ride, and the incomparable musical drive of the Royal Horse Artillery, their six gleaming gun-carriages now in line together, now separating to the corners of the arena for the notorious 'scissors', when they raced diagonally towards and past one another hub to hub with barely the width of a horseshoe between.

Most of the ingredients of the now legendary Naval Field Gun Competition had come together in 1907 when teams from two home ports first raced each other to manhandle more than a ton of ordnance over obstacles. The competition quickly settled into its familiar format. Eighteen-man teams trained for months against the stopwatch to run a gun and limber to the base of a 5ft-high wall, dismantle them, rig a sheerlegs and secure a wire jackstay across a 30ft 'chasm', hitch themselves to the wire

Archery for the first (and last) time at Olympia. Bright sun through the glass roof 'had a rather perplexing effect on the targets', 1906. (Royal Toxophilite Society Register)

Programme printed on silk for Olympia's inaugural event, the Paris Hippodrome, which opened on 26 December 1886. *(K. Whitehouse collection)*

Official Guide, medallion and a 1s admission ticket for Earls Court showground's inaugural event, the Amerian Exhibition, opened on 9 May 1887. *(K. Whitehouse collection)* Attendant's punch-card entry pass. *(A. Smith collection)*

Transfer-printed china, c. 1890. *(K. Whitehouse collection)*

Bolossy Kiralfy's 'Constantinople', Olympia 1893/4.
(K. Whitehouse collection)

Olympia's second SMMT Motor Show, 1905. (ECO)

Buffalo Bill's Wild West Co. promotional envelope, Earls Court, 1892. (K. Whitehouse collection)

Above, left: The Welcome Club, Earls Court, established 1887. *Above, right: top, left to right:* The Gigantic Wheel, cheap medallion (reverse), 1897; Royal Tournament, medallion, undated but post-1919. *Bottom:* The Gigantic Wheel, cheap medallion (obverse), 1897; The Italian Exhibition, souvenir medal, Earls Court, 1904; International Exhibition of Ancient Art, commemorative medal, Earls Court, 1911; Royal Naval & Military Tournament, 1st Prize RM Artillery bayonet team, Olympia, 1912. *(K. Whitehouse collection)*

The Gigantic Wheel, transfer-printed china, Earls Court, c. 1900. *(K. Whitehouse collection)*

Commemorative china, Earls Court. *Front*: Shakespeare's England, 1912. *Rear, left to right*: Anglo-Spanish Travel Exhibition, 1914; Golden West Exhibition, 1909; Imperial Services Exhibition, 1913. *(K. Whitehouse collection)*

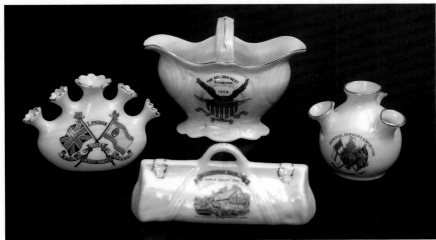

Above: International Fire Exhibition, season ticket for owner and guest, Earls Court, 1903. *(K. Whitehouse collection)*

Left: International Fire Exhibition, 1903. *(Hammersmith & Fulham Archives)*

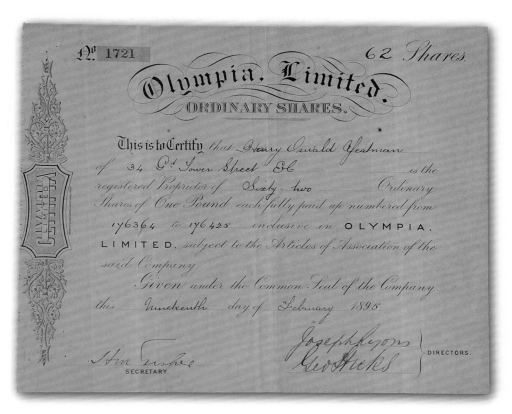

Olympia Ltd share certificate issued over Joe Lyons' signature, February 1895. The company crashed in July. *(K. Whitehouse collection)*

Cochran's miracle – 'The Miracle', Olympia, 1911/12. *(ECO)*

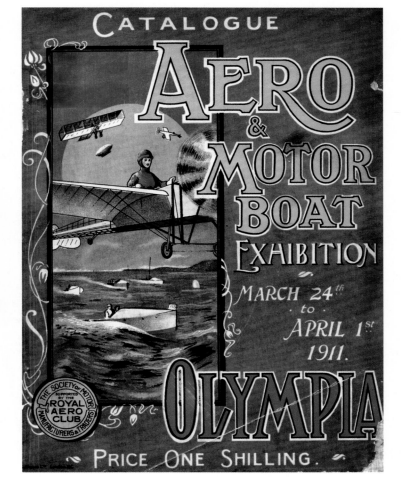

Surprisingly, this was a Society of Motor Manufacturers & Trader's show. Olympia, 1911. *(ECO)*

IMPERIAL SERVICES EXHIBITION
EMPRESS HALL   EARLS COURT. 1913
Naval & Aerial Warfare

PART I *Peace*   PART II *War*

OFFICIAL PROGRAMME
AND GUIDE 6ᴰ (NET

Above, left: The prescient Imperial Services Exhibition, Earls Court, 1913. *(K. Whitehouse collection)*
Right: Top: A very fine early Empress Theatre ticket for 'Savage South Africa', 1899.
Centre: Bandsman's pass, Italian Exhibition, Earls Court, 1904. *Bottom:* Admission to the
Imperial Services Exhibition grounds. The ticket secures a discount for the Empress Hall
show. *(A. Smith collection)*
Left & below: International Horse Show, 1st prize rosette and show poster, Olympia, 1910.
(left, K. Whitehouse collection; below, ECO)

(ECO)

(ECO)

Earls Court shares
option over Frank
Lewis' signature,
July 1937.

(K. Whitehouse collection)

OFFICIAL CATALOGUE.   Price 6d.

BUILDING EXHIBITION
OLYMPIA.

THE HOUSE BEAUTIFUL.

APRIL 12th to 26th, 1913.

(ECO)

BOSTOCK'S THREE RING CIRCUS
Empress Hall, Earl's Court, London.
1928~9

(K. Whitehouse collection)

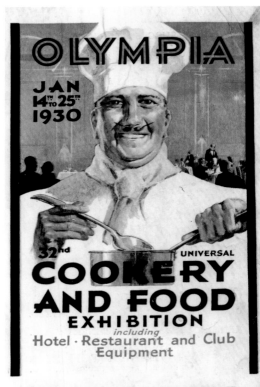

OLYMPIA
JAN 14TH TO 25TH 1930

32nd UNIVERSAL
COOKERY AND FOOD EXHIBITION
including
Hotel · Restaurant and Club Equipment

OFFICIAL CATALOGUE
PRICE ONE SHILLING

(ECO)

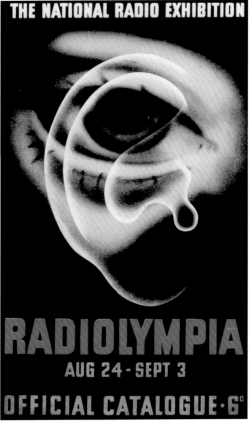

THE NATIONAL RADIO EXHIBITION

RADIOLYMPIA
AUG 24 - SEPT 3
OFFICIAL CATALOGUE · 6D

1938 (ECO)

and cross the void clutching achingly heavy and sweat-slippery artillery wheels and all the rest before reassembling the gun and limber and dashing to a finishing line to fire off one round. After a gasping pause the contestants raced back the way they had come, the first over the start line being awarded one point. A trophy went to the team with the highest point score over the run of the Tournament. Time penalties were given for infringements.

By 1914 the Tournament was almost entirely spectacle and music, the competition side being relegated to morning sessions to which interested members of the public were admitted for a small charge. The First World War broke out just weeks later and the Tournament did not return to Olympia until June 1919. Few of those who took part in the previous show would have lived to see it.

Two big new shows – and sweated labour

Archery came to Olympia in March 1906 for the first – and apparently last – time. An important open competition was shot there but *The Times* reported that brilliant sunshine through the glass roof 'had a rather perplexing effect on the targets'.

Left: Hugh Greville Montgomery, founder of the Building Trades Exhibition in 1895. It came to Olympia in 1905 and continued under three generations of the Montgomery family. *(Montgomery Exhibitions)*

Right: A corner of Montgomery's Building Exhibition, c. 1910. It outgrew Olympia and moved to the NEC in 1977. *(Montgomery Exhibitions)*

Reginald Heaton, urbane founder of Olympia's International Horse Show in 1907. He became MD of Olympia in 1912, retiring in 1947 after a 40-year association with the halls. (ECO)

The International Building Trades Exhibition transferred from the Aggie the next year. Renamed Interbuild in 1973, it remains one of Britain's largest and most successful trade shows and is certainly the longest-running. It was conceived at the Islington hall in 1894, the result of a £500 deal between the organiser of the ramshackle 'Building Exhibition' then taking place and Hugh Greville Montgomery, a dissatisfied exhibitor. The event was a hybrid collection of goods, many of which had no connection whatsoever with the building trades. Young Montgomery, editor of a trade periodical, so impressed the organiser that he was offered a partnership.

After a £500 deal the organiser dropped out, leaving Montgomery to rebuild the exhibition into an authoritative trade event with the support of his brother 'Stow'. Wanting it to be 'more than a mere show', he introduced daily conferences, demonstrations of craftsmanship and the testing of materials. The restructured exhibition was launched at the Aggie in March 1895 and was an immediate success. It ran on there as a biennial event until in 1905, with 317 exhibitors and a waiting list, it had to move. It continued at Olympia from 1907 under the direction of three generations of the Montgomery family, going to Birmingham's NEC in 1977 when it finally outgrew its London home.

Many equestrian events have passed through Olympia, but the First International Horse Show which followed Montgomery's Building Exhibition in June 1907 was a trail-blazer. Hitherto, such events were for the horsey fraternity and were patronised almost exclusively by men. Reginald Heaton, a farmer and horse breeder, and four friends put up £2,500 to stage a show which would appeal to 'society' and become part of the social calendar – an indoor Ascot. Lord Lonsdale was its president and the very able Heaton was managing director of the organising company.

The arena was turfed and rather over-generously planted with trees, flower beds and shrubs – the florist's bill a year or so later came to £6,000. Over two thousand horses were entered, including several hundred from the USA. On the opening day 20,000 visitors packed in. After daily competitions and diversions the Coaching Club held a special meet at Hyde Park on the closing day, the teams then driving to Olympia to compete for a gold cup for the best turnout. The week was an instant success and it became another of Pa Payne's annual 'banker' shows, especially welcome in the fallow summer season.

A coaching marathon ('race' to most contestants) was included in subsequent shows. The route from Bushey Park gates at Hampton Court to Olympia was always lined with thousands of cheering spectators. Entries were confined to working road coaches carrying at least seven people including a show official. The rules stated:

In the event of a coach desiring to pass the one ahead of it, the coachman of the latter must allow the following coach to do so if the leaders of that coach reach his

hind wheel. The coachman of the coach being thus passed must not in any way pull his team across or obstruct the right of way of the approaching coach. In the event of the coachman of the following coach being unable, on reaching the hind wheel, to pass within two minutes, the official representative of the leading coach will sign him to pull behind again.... The competitors must only pass each other at a trot.

The 1910 line-up of six coaches included the favourite, Mr Vanderbilt's famous greys of the Brighton Venture; Mr Barron of the Hampton Court Venture with a 'workmanlike' team; the Eastbourne & Brighton Vigilant; the Tantivy from Esher; and the Old Times which ran daily to Oatlands Park at Weybridge, driven by Mr G.K. Fownes, the doyen of professional whips, with a magnificent team of blacks. The greatest problem was obstruction from unsympathetic motorists en route. The International Horse Show became as firm a favourite as the circus.

Pre-war gatherings of the establishment became targets of the Women's Social & Political Union, the well-organised militant suffragette wing of the wider movement for women's rights and the vote. One of its objectives was the abolition of the evils of sweated female labour and the appalling conditions in which too many women worked. Emily Davison's tragic suicide at the Epsom Derby in 1913 when she ran beneath the flying hooves of the king's horse was an extreme example of their defiant militancy.

The Horse Show's coaching marathon from Bushey to Olympia (11¼m), c. 1912. The Royal Box is a very grand construction. (ECO)

A disturbance at the 1914 Horse Show was directed at the king. He had just entered the royal box when a woman in a distant corner near the Annexe jumped up and shrilly appealed, 'Your Majesty, why do you allow torture of women . . .' – the band hastily struck up and a spectator grabbed the woman as the police arrived to take her away, to cheers and counter-cheers from the pro and anti sections of the capacity audience. Peace followed for a time before half a dozen others tried at intervals to repeat the cry and were duly removed, this time to loud hissing and booing.

Lloyd George, Chancellor of the Exchequer, had suffered a similar verbal assault at close quarters on leaving the Olympia Motor Show the year before. The National Anti Sweating League also had a stand at Olympia's 1913 Kinematograph Exhibition. A rather different health and safety exhibit there comprised a French-built 'Kinematographic Cabin' for the projectionist. A water cylinder was fitted on the roof because of the fire risk from highly flammable acetate film. In an emergency the operator could pull a chain to release a spray – if he was not already half-way to the door.

The Ideal Home Exhibition

'The foundations of the national glory are set in the Homes of the People.' When King George V spoke these words he intended a rather deeper meaning than the *Daily Mail*'s interpretation. The paper nevertheless set about the practical business of promoting home-making, and in the process it created something of a national treasure.

The *Daily Mail* Ideal Home Exhibition was the longest-running of all Olympia's events, and it continues at Earls Court. Since the show's inception in 1908 it has mirrored social change and influenced public taste. In the first decades of the twentieth century many had little spare cash for even the basic necessities of the home. To them the show would have seemed a palace of dreams. Times changed, and increased spending power and extended credit have long since transformed the domestic economy. Dreams became hopes, and hopes are now expectations. The earnest and rather preachy 'Ideal Homes' of the early years were blown away by the First World War's impact on society at all levels. It developed a sense of humour and lightness of touch which has stayed with it.

The idea originated with Wareham Smith, a director of Lord Northcliffe's Associated Newspapers and advertising manager of the *Daily Mail*. He saw it as a profitable operation in its own right, as well as a powerful circulation and advertising builder. The exhibition was pitched at those who populated the great mass of new housing surrounding the capital, and at the many who aspired to join them.

The first *Daily Mail* Ideal Home Exhibition opened on Friday 9 October 1908. It was presented as a living manual of advice, services and household goods in twelve themed sections including how to build and equip the home, the baby in the home, hygiene and cleaning, the garden and home work. A welcoming military band inevitably played *Home Sweet Home*. The newspaper had run an architects' competition for the best-designed cottage in three price-bands. Plans and sketches from nearly 450 entries were displayed on the gallery, to be judged by Sir Edwin Lutyens. Visitors were invited to give

Evelyn Hardy's band at the Ideal Home Exhibition, Olympia, 1913. *(H&FA)*

Home sweet home at the 1st Daily Mail Ideal Home Exhibition, Olympia, 1908. This historic photograph records the first of the many full-scale houses that would feature in succeeding years. *(Daily Mail)*

their own opinion in a parallel competition, and to furnish the design of their choice from items displayed at the show.

Booths of gadgets, remedies and equipment for immediate purchase lined the remoter gangways. Ladies were offered 'Hercules' corset stiffeners, able to withstand the wearer's domestic bending and stooping which snapped rival brands. Gentlemen could ride away on a sturdy Enfield bicycle 'made like a gun' for only £5 9s. Elsewhere entirely hand-operated wooden-tub 'washing machines' were offered with gears and ball bearings, at £8 including stand. The 'Pneuvac' bucket and mop was just that, the only pneumatic and vacuum properties being those of the user.

Charles B. 'Cockie' Cochran, the impresario who brought wrestling, boxing, circuses and ambitious theatre to Olympia. (AC)

The exhibition's centrepiece was invariably as ambitious as space and a generous budget allowed. Memorable among them were scale replicas of the sixteenth-century Palace of Fontainebleau and the presidential White House. The centrepiece later merged with the exhibition's traditional cluster of full-size show-houses. These appeared as early as the 1910 event when the organisers built a Tudor village across the back of the Annexe. The row of timbered cottages fronted a very grassy green and pond, the unsightly iron roof supports being transformed into avenues of mature oaks of singularly uniform girth and upright habit.

Deborah Ryan in her *The Ideal Home through the 20th Century* (Hazar Publishing, 1997) points to the overwhelming popularity of the mock-Tudor or 'Tudorbethan' style as applied especially to new semi-detached homes. They were generally well built in slightly contrasting styles to avoid uniformity, using modern materials with good-quality fittings, and set with mass-produced 'Jacobethan' furniture. The vogue lasted from this period right up to 1939, its popularity arising in part from its distinctively different appearance from local authority council estates of plain neo-Georgian form.

The show houses must be the most common memory of the millions who have visited the exhibition since 1908. The concept of a cluster of full-scale buildings in stock materials and in superbly landscaped settings in the middle of a vast and colourful exhibition is in the Kiralfy class. Typically, the prize-winning 'Ideal House' of 1912, a brick-built home of nine fully fitted rooms furnished by Barkers of Kensington, was built in nine-and-a-half days from 250 tons of building materials.

Miracle – and nightmare

As a boy, Charles Cochran had seen one of Kiralfy's productions at Olympia. It so impressed him that he vowed one day to do something there himself, he knew not what, but it would be on heroic lines. His 'The Miracle' was all of that. It was the most lavishly equipped and ambitious theatrical spectacle ever to be staged there. Such a production could not be repeated today. Its costs would be of seismic proportions, not to mention the unthinkable damage done to the hall's floor and sub-structure.

Cochran hated the way a theatre's proscenium arch formed a barrier to intimacy between actors and audience, believing the open ring of the circus to be vastly superior. After seeing the great German producer Max Reinhardt's *Oedipus Rex* in Berlin in the summer of 1909 he determined that Reinhardt should produce an Olympia spectacle for him, but what? At a chance meeting there, the young poet-dramatist Karl Volmöller gave Cochran a scenario worthy of so vast an auditorium. It was suffused with Germanic medieval myth and legend.

The epic story, almost entirely in dumb-show because of Olympia's size, centres on a nun who is left one evening to lock up a great cathedral, only to fall into a reverie in which she dreams of the temptations of the world outside. She is swept away by a knight and suffers adventures, humiliation and worse. The cathedral's statue of the Madonna comes alive in her place, guarding the building until the nun's return as a penitent, driven back there by a mob to her protective fellow priests, from whom she receives forgiveness. This hardly does justice to the production's powerful emotions and depth of meaning, and the broad canvas of processions, hunting parties, marches to battle and amazing scene changes from the cathedral interior to tree-clad mountain slopes. The cast was huge. The production was allegorical, and intended to be viewed in a spirit of detachment, much as one would regard a painting or poetry. It was a brave new approach to theatre.

Fired with Volmöller's vision, Cochran took a train to Budapest to meet Reinhardt. On the way he imagined Olympia as a cathedral, a great rose window at each end, with towering columns and clever lighting for the medieval mystery play. The two men talked through the night, Reinhardt warming to the idea. They parted as collaborators. Next stop was Pa Payne, who smelt success and proposed – to Cockie's astonishment – that Olympia should put up all the money in return for half the profits, the other half to be divided equally between himself and Cochran. Cockie at once agreed the deal. 'The Miracle' was to open on Christmas Eve 1911. Humperdinck, composer of *Hansel and Gretl*, agreed to write the score.

Reinhardt's art director was the imperturbable genius Professor Ernst Stern, who designed everything from the 2,000 costumes to the cathedral interior which he based on Cologne. Asked by Cochran what on earth could be done to transform Olympia's iron trusses and acres of glass into a Gothic cathedral, Stern replied: 'You are never stuck for theatrical illusion so long as you have black material and black paint.'

Auditioning for the nun was pure pantomime. The volatile Russian dancer Natacha Trouhanowa begged for the part, offering to travel to Germany to give a demonstration. Cochran, Reinhardt and Volmöller accompanied her to Humperdinck's small cottage miles from Munich, where the party was received coolly by Frau Humperdinck after noting the dancer's Parisian turnout. Trouhanowa retired to change, returning to the small sitting room wearing little more than a diaphanous silken garment and a cloud of perfume. Frau Humperdinck sent her teenage son straight to bed and ordered Professor Humperdinck to keep his back to the siren while he played the piano and she gyrated, cavorted and high-kicked. A picture fell from the wall. China shook. The men watching were transfixed. The lady won the part.

Selection of the Madonna was equally challenging. The award went at Cockie's urging to the strikingly beautiful Frau Volmöller who had never acted before but who proved an outstanding success. Billed as Maria Carmi, she was required to be a lime-lit golden

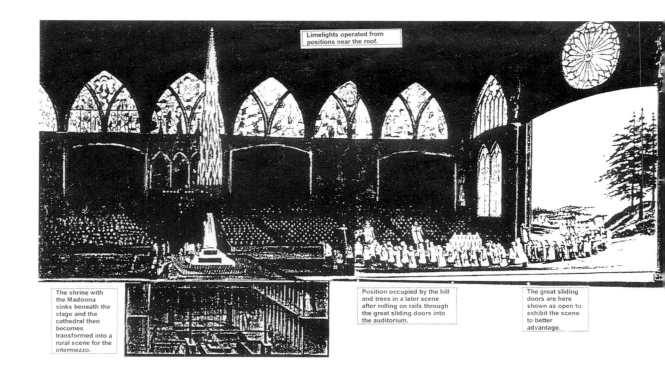

Limelights operated from positions near the roof.

The shrine with the Madonna sinks beneath the stage and the cathedral then becomes transformed into a rural scene for the intermezzo.

Position occupied by the hill and trees in a later scene after rolling on rails through the great sliding doors into the auditorium.

The great sliding doors are here shown as open to exhibit the scene to better advantage.

Olympia's interior became a cathedral for Cochran's ruinously extravagant 'The Miracle' in 1911-12. Note the huge pit specially excavated beneath the hydraulically raised and lowered stage, and the tree-clad hill which rolled into the auditorium on rails for an arcadian scene-change. *(ECO)*

Madonna on a high pedestal for some forty-five minutes, unmoving as the action took place around her. Suddenly she comes alive, stepping down to the utter incredulity of the audience, moved by the emotional scene. It was superb theatre which lost nothing by the fact that later audiences knew what was coming. They dared not take their eyes off her for fear of missing that first or any premature movement.

Olympia was in use until 10 December, leaving a bare fortnight in which to transform the place before rehearsing 1,000 performers and 500 choristers. A dramatic scene of burning at the stake called for a huge trap the size of the Drury Lane stage to be cut through the hall floor and a void excavated beneath. Hydraulic machinery was installed there to raise and lower the stage. In a striking simulation the victim would descend silently through fire into the depths, engulfed in 'flames' of silken streamers blown vertical by fans below. The platform bearing the Madonna and others would also descend out of sight in dimmed lighting for a major scene change as a tree-covered hill glided into the hall from the Annexe end on unseen rails, changing the auditorium into a sunlit rural setting as the lights came up. Meanwhile, Volmöller and her fellow actors would make their way through an underground passage from the pit to backstage.

Steam cranes were still working in the building during the final dress rehearsal. Many miles of power cable snaked about the floor and over cable bridges, and dozens of lighting trusses had been rigged. Transmission of the stream of lighting cues to the electricians across the vastness of Olympia meant wiring up cue-lamps to points all over the hall. In the event it all went perfectly on opening night and the audience was thrilled.

Press reviews were good, but not good enough to boost attendances at the twice-daily performances. They averaged 5,000 – half the capacity. Weekly running expenses were slightly in excess of receipts; Cochran needed full houses. Ten days later he got them, thanks to Lord Northcliffe's support through the *Daily Mail*. Ironically, it was the paper which was also the show's undoing. 'The Miracle' had to close on 2 March to make way for the Ideal Home Exhibition, just when capacity audiences were achieved. Cockie had hoped to get an extension to the 16th.

'The Miracle' became nightmare. Olympia had secured a mortgage of £11,000 to underpin its contribution, but it lost nearly £20,000. It was too much for the company and that August the hall changed hands yet again. Olympia (1912) Ltd was formed with Sir Gilbert Greenall as chairman, with a new board. Pa Payne returned to Allsopps and, sadly, has been long forgotten. Payne's misjudgement should be set against his encouragement of the specialist trade exhibitions and his early decision to build Olympia's business around them, so setting its course for years ahead. By the time Payne left he had secured and hosted events covering the electrical, engineering and machinery, mining, mercantile marine, rubber and oil, hardware and office equipment industries, and business and advertising services. The change of direction was a defining moment, and his lasting contribution.

Reginald Heaton from the International Horse Show replaced Payne as managing director. He was an urbane professional, fastidious in his dress and with the charm and manners of the Edwardian gentleman. He sold his farm and stud for £12,000 in order

'The Miracle'. Olympia's transformation by stage designer Ernest Stern is clear. *(British Library: Pall Mall Magazine, January 1912)*

to take up Sir Gilbert's invitation to join him at Olympia. Heaton's first event was a funeral. The death of General Booth of the Salvation Army had brought more than 100,000 mourners to Clapton to pay their respects at the lying in state. The coffin was then taken to an absolutely packed Olympia for the funeral on 28 August 1912.

Monkey business

After the extravagances of 'The Miracle', the following Christmas tenancy went from high drama to low budget with a modest and unmemorable Children's Welfare Exhibition. Cochran then reappeared to ask Heaton for an option for 1913/14. He had been impressed by the 'natural' zoo of explorer Carl Hagenbeck of Hamburg, who wrote: 'I desired above all things to give animals the maximum of liberty, not as captives but as free as possible to wander.' In place of cages he gave his animals large areas in more or less natural surroundings, separated from spectators by trenches. Cochran proposed a similar treatment at Olympia, combined with a large circus. He won his option and, after considerable difficulty, found the necessary backers.

Hagenbeck's two-month 'Wonder Zoo and Big Circus' was a stupendous affair with 1,000 animals and birds. On the right of the main hall on entering one saw lions, apparently running free on a mountainside. Along the left wall the most popular display of the show were 500 Barbary apes, also uncaged and separated only by a trench. In the centre of the hall was a 5,000-seat circus with what Cockie considered to be the finest programme ever performed in a single ring. Acts included the 250 liberty horses of the Corthy-Althoffs; the Flying Rainats acrobats who set their trapezes swinging at right angles to each other, a dangerous movement; May Worth, star rider of Barnum's circus; and many more. In the first two days 63,000 people paid at the turnstiles. Additionally, the circus took £1,000 a day. In late February the millionth visitor received a £10 note (six times the weekly wage of a farm labourer).

The show was not without incident. Moritz, one of a pair of performing chimpanzees, finished his skating turn, then pushed over the barrier and climbed into the royal box. Luckily it was empty but he bit ring attendant Sidney Pratt on the chin before blacking his eye. Pratt won £50 damages. Much more serious was the poisoning of four horses in the stables, belonging to three different acts. One was a very valuable white stallion owned by Baptista Schreiber, an attractive and accomplished Danish rider. The culprit was never caught. A fund was organised and Baptista was presented with a new horse at a special performance attended by Princess Alexandra. Two of the horses survived the attack, which involved cayenne pepper. When the Wonder Zoo prepared to depart, numbers of monkeys clambered into the higher reaches of the roof fearlessly pursued by keepers, while Carlo the giant ostrich made several high-speed circuits of the building. Hagenbeck's Wonder Zoo and Circus was to be Olympia's last Christmas entertainment before the outbreak of the First World War which destroyed so many, and so much of the Old England.

FIVE

EARLS COURT
Glory Days

'It is very gratifying to me to think . . . that I may have helped to raise the standard of spectacular entertainment, and that I have contributed something to the artistic needs as well as to the gaiety of nations.'

Imre Kiralfy, originator of many great productions at Earls Court and Olympia between 1891 and 1906, Strand Magazine, 1909

IMRE KIRALFY'S 'VENICE' at Olympia ended its thirteen-month run in January 1893. He had already departed to produce 'America', a grand historical pageant for the Chicago World's Fair later that year. It was inevitably on an unprecedented scale matched only by the take at the turnstiles. Kiralfy was well rewarded, and now turned his energies to Earls Court. He had declined a generous offer from John Whitley to produce the arena show for the German Exhibition in 1891, convinced that nothing could be done with the venue unless it was secured on a long lease, laid out afresh and completely rebuilt.

Kiralfy persuaded the District Railway to give him an option on the showground and in the summer of 1894 invited Harold Hartley to help him form an operating company. Hartley was a director of Olympia Ltd at that time and remained so until its liquidation in July 1895. He raised £100,000 and the option was taken up for a 21-year lease from the end of 1894 (later extended to 42 years). Leading supporter Paul Cremieu-Javal of caterers Spiers & Pond was appointed chairman of London Exhibitions Ltd with Kiralfy its director-general. Cremieu-Javal found the artistic Hungarian difficult to work with and urged Hartley to stand between them as managing director. Hartley held the appointment for sixteen very productive years.

The company set about a total reconstruction of the showground. There was no chance of completion before the following year so Milner and Dodson were recalled to put on an Industrial Exhibition in 1894 as a 'filler'. The immediate surroundings rapidly became a building site. A 264ft-high Ferris wheel at the 1893 Chicago Exposition was echoed in the 300ft-high 40-car version which was built at Earls Court. (The London Eye tops 450ft.) Kiralfy was not directly concerned with Earls Court's Gigantic Wheel, which began construction in March 1894. Society columnist Ouida acidly observed that, 'the fact that the great wheel of Earls Court should attract sane persons as a diversion will alone prove how completely the instinct of correct taste, with its accompanying abhorrence of deformity, has become

extinct in all modern crowds.' *The Graphic* took the contrary view, declaring the Wheel to be 'A Revolution'.

The 6,000-seat Empress Hall replaced Whitley's temporary building on the centre island. Beyond it the large open Imperial Court was encircled by a covered display gallery. At Kiralfy's urging the Albert Palace buildings in Battersea Park, originally designed for the 1865 Dublin Exhibition, were purchased for re-erection as Earls Court's exhibition halls. It was then found that they could not be put on the site because of their enormous weight on the unstable ground. They were sold for scrap at considerable loss. The old Hippodrome in Paris was bought instead. Re-erected across the west end of the Kensington triangle fronting Boyton's lake, it was renamed the Queen's Hall. It blew down in a March gale in 1895 before it had been completed.

With two large buildings already written off and the ambitious Empire of India Exhibition due to open in May, Harold Hartley found himself fighting a board decision to postpone the show for a year. He knew that the company's credibility and now ruinous finances could not withstand such delay – and he carried the day. The wrecked Hippodrome was removed and the site became an instant garden with bandstand, surrounded by a surviving colonnade of white pillars above small shops.

The exhibition was opened on 10 May 1896 by the Duke of Cambridge. The Gigantic Wheel was tested and cleared for public use on 3 July. The theatre opened on 24 August for Kiralfy's 'Indian Spectacle'. Showground general foreman Edwin Smith took his young son up into the roof, hoping to get him used to heights. As an

Opposite: Earls Court's Gigantic Wheel, 1896–1906. The immensely popular and – literally – revolutionary 300ft-high wheel carried 1,200 passengers at a time. *(RBKC)*

Earls Court's exhibition grounds were rebuilt in 1896 for the Empire of India Exhibition. Note the new Empress Theatre (*left*), the water chute backing on to Lillie Road (*foreground*) and the lake and ornate buildings in the old 'triangle'. The Gigantic Wheel looms distantly in this unique panorama of 1900. *(ECO)*

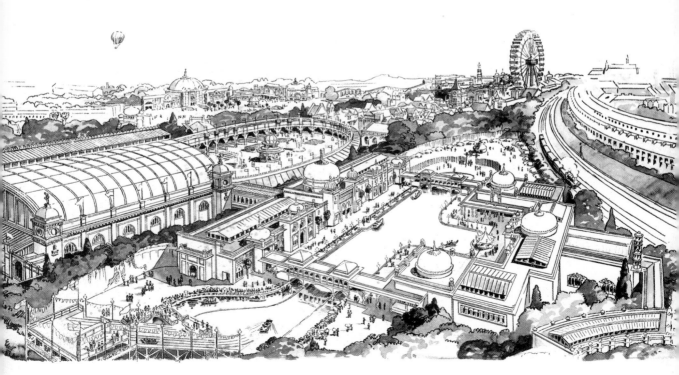

No ordinary railway footbridge. The Western Gardens entrance to the Long Bridge or Western Arcade which crossed to the central island and the Empress Theatre, Earls Court, 1904. It was built in 1894/5. *(RBKC)*

ex-mariner who had sailed in windjammers round Cape Horn Smith had no fears, but the lad never forgot the experience and remained a groundling.

The Empress Theatre was Kiralfy's personal fiefdom, its highly unorthodox interior layout custom-built for his spectaculars. As with his 'Venice' at Olympia, the key elements – seating, pool and stage – were aligned lengthways, the seats running in a single tier the entire length of the theatre. The stage, 315ft wide beneath an enormous proscenium arch, incorporated stepped platforms which could be withdrawn to reveal a large expanse of water. Between the seats and the stage was a shallow concrete water tank approximately an acre in size which doubled as a dry arena. The orchestra was elevated and hidden from spectators behind the proscenium. All scenery was suspended.

Architect Allan O. Collard's economical iron-framed structure was clad with concrete slabs under a corrugated iron roof on bowstring girders to provide a clear span. He may have originated Kiralfy's subsequent lavishly ornamented buildings in the triangle, the Queen's Palace exhibition hall along the west end of the old arena, and the Ducal Hall at the Warwick Road end which faced it across Boyton's lake.

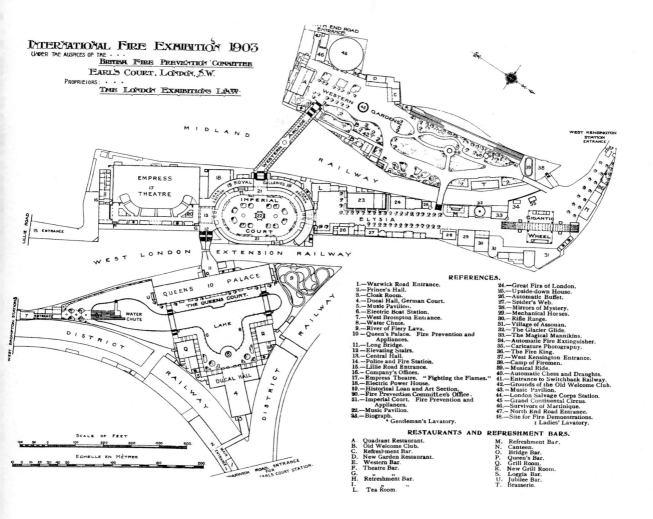

INTERNATIONAL FIRE EXHIBITION 1903

UNDER THE AUSPICES OF THE · · ·
BRITISH FIRE PREVENTION COMMITTEE
EARL'S COURT, LONDON, S.W.
PROPRIETORS : · · ·
THE LONDON EXHIBITIONS LIMITED

REFERENCES.

1.—Warwick Road Entrance.
3.—Prince's Hall.
3.—Cloak Room.
4.—Ducal Hall, German Court.
5.—Music Pavilion.
6.—Electric Boat Station.
7.—West Brompton Entrance.
8.—Water Chute.
9.—River of Fiery Lava.
10.—Queen's Palace. Fire Prevention and Appliances.
11.—Long Bridge.
12.—Elevating Stairs.
13.—Central Hall.
14.—Police and Fire Station.
15.—Lillie Road Entrance.
16.—Company's Offices.
17.—Empress Theatre. "Fighting the Flames."
18.—Electric Power House.
19.—Historical Loan and Art Section.
20.—Fire Prevention Committee's Office.
21.—Imperial Court. Fire Prevention and Appliances.
22.—Music Pavilion.
23.—Biograph.
* Gentleman's Lavatory.

24.—Great Fire of London.
25.—Upside-down House.
26.—Automatic Buffet.
27.—Spider's Web.
28.—Mirrors of Mystery.
29.—Mechanical Horses.
30.—Rifle Range.
31.—Village of Assouan.
32.—The Glacier Glide.
33.—The Magical Mannikins.
34.—Automatic Fire Extinguisher.
35.—Caricature Photography.
36.—The Fire King.
37.—West Kensington Entrance.
38.—Camp of Firemen.
39.—Musical Ride.
40.—Automatic Chess and Draughts.
41.—Entrance to Switchback Railway.
42.—Grounds of the Old Welcome Club.
43.—Music Pavilion.
44.—London Salvage Corps Station.
45.—Grand Continental Circus.
46.—Survivors of Martinique.
47.—North End Road Entrance.
48.—Site for Fire Demonstrations.
‡ Ladies' Lavatory.

RESTAURANTS AND REFRESHMENT BARS.

A Quadrant Restaurant.
B. Old Welcome Club.
C. Refreshment Bar.
D. New Garden Restaurant.
E. Western Bar.
F. Theatre Bar.
G. " "
H. Refreshment Bar.
I.
L. Tea Room. "

M. Refreshment Bar.
N. Canteen.
O. Bridge Bar.
P. Queen's Bar.
Q. Grill Room.
R. New Grill Room.
S. Loggia Bar.
U. Jubilee Bar.
T. Brasserie.

For the India Exhibition Kiralfy turned the theatre into a miniature Indian court, filled with ornate detailing and colour. As always, he let his audience feel they were learning something of value while he dazzled them with masterly showmanship. A pageant comprised re-enactments of events in India's history from a rather colonial standpoint. A drama centred on a heroic widow on her husband's funeral pyre who spurns offers of safety from a Brahmin intent on securing other favours. As the flames and smoke rise higher she rather fortunately falls through a secret trap door into a chamber where she turns into an idol in a sea of precious stones. She is only restored to life when discovered by a heroic conqueror. Much treachery follows before the climax is reached, with dancing girls giving shapely confirmation that the two have reached Paradise.

The 'Old Welcome Club' was revived in the Western Gardens under the presidency of Field-Marshal Lord 'Bobs' Roberts, becoming once more a rendezvous for much of London society.

The attractions of Lord George Sanger's circus provided an alternative to the ornate palaces and crowded bazaars, peopled with Benares coppersmiths, weavers of silks and sellers of carpets, snake-charmers and fakirs. After an embarrassing encounter between Sanger and London County Council inspectors the circus opening was delayed for several days. Was the big marquee flame-proof? 'Certainly, one hundred per

A rare view of the main entrance in Warwick Road, opposite Earls Court underground station, during the Imperial Royal Austrian Exhibition, 1906. Contrast this with the photograph of today's Earls Court on page 131 taken from almost the same camera position. The 1906 structure straddles the present centre gates. (H&FA)

Earls Court's Old Welcome Club became a fashionable rendezvous in the Western Gardens for London's notables and socialites. Harold Hartley is standing (*in top hat, far right*) with Mrs Hartley. (*Arthur Smith collection*)

cent.' A match was applied to a corner – and the canvas burned as furiously as Sanger's cheeks.

The 1,100-ton Gigantic Wheel stood behind West Kensington station at the far end of the central island. Its forty cars each seated thirty passengers: 1,200 in all. Ten cars were furnished as saloons with easy chairs and settees where tea, coffee and ice-cream were served.

Departure for the twenty-minute ride is signalled by the locking of the door from the outside and much blowing of whistles. Then the near-silent ascent, the ground appearing to collapse away rather than any impression of rising oneself. An intermittent metallic creak is the only mechanical sound. The 16-ton drive-chains on either side, 1,000ft long, move silently under huge load from their Robey steam engines. The wheel stops occasionally for several cars at a time to discharge passengers and let others board. A sudden realisation on looking up through the vast steel web of beams and braces to the sky beyond that one is now slightly worryingly high; entirely dependent on this encircling mass of metal to hang together long enough for us to get down. Olympia's 450ft-long roof appears as a mere greenhouse to the north. Windsor

Castle is visible on a clear day at 16 miles. The panjandrum stops again, the carriage momentarily swaying a little at the top of the cycle. Oddly, every note of the band nearly 300ft below sounds clear, but flattened somehow. One can almost hear the rattle of china as white-jacketed waiters with afternoon tea on silver trays hurry across the lawn of the Old Welcome Club, their striding legs foreshortened to purposeful stumps. Then the descent, and for the first time a sensation of vibrant motion, as if the wheel is resisting. Strange to slide groundward towards roofs of moving trains. We leave the car at the far end of the high boarding platform, feeling much as a voyager departing a ship. Mild elation with a hint of unsteadiness, and a determination to do it again – soon.

The Wheel got stuck just before 9pm on 21 May 1896 with sixty or seventy passengers aboard. They remained suspended between earth and sky until noon the following day, ex-sailor attendants bravely climbing the frames to reach them with refreshment and reassurance. The Guards Band stayed late into the evening to

The Wheel under construction. It stuck in 1896 with sixty or seventy passengers aboard. They remained suspended between earth and sky until noon the following day, attendants bravely climbing the frames to reach them with refreshment and reassurance. (GHL, The Graphic)

entertain the castaways who each received £5 5s in compensation – a substantial sum in those days. When word of the payment got out next day *The Graphic* estimated that 11,000 people queued for a ride, many hoping for another failure. All would have got aboard – the record carried in one day stood at 13,328. After conveying an estimated 2.5 million passengers, the Wheel was taken down by George Cohen of Stepney in the winter of 1906/7 and cut up for scrap.

Days of wonder

W. Macqueen-Pope has described the old Earls Court Exhibition as 'having the witchery of magic'. It was indeed a place of dreams and enchantment, drama and entertainment for millions. This was its Golden Age. The mammoth and hugely popular shows ran on into the new century like a line of boxcars. There were many highlights.

Cremieu-Javal, whose company now held the catering concession for Earls Court, kept strict control of the showground's finances which 'India' had restored to health. Hartley travelled widely, visiting major foreign exhibitions to assess new productions and speciality acts, and building contacts for future shows. He also managed all the promotion and public travel arrangements. Kiralfy laid on the theatre productions, big spectacles and amusements. Crucially, he designed and managed the stunning architectural and decorative transformations each year which reflected the theme of the show. They had one basic rule: each exhibition should run for twenty-one weeks or more, and annual costs should not exceed £500 per exhibition open day.

'India' was so popular that it was continued for another year with added features from Ceylon, Borneo and Burma. Hartley's travels secured a two-year monopoly on distorting mirrors, an unheard-of novelty. Rickshaws were introduced for rides around the grounds and remained an attraction for many years.

The show marked a change in emphasis since Whitley's day. Entertainment for him had been secondary, a means to a largely educational end. Kiralfy and Hartley reversed this while ensuring that the highest standards were maintained throughout. Their large

Balloon ascent at the Earls Court exhibition ground, 1898. *(GHL, The Graphic)*

'static' exhibitions were well researched and reinforced with live demonstrations whenever possible. Much use was made of popular dioramas, pantomimographs, cycloramas and magic lantern-type projections. Kiralfy's spectaculars too were invariably informative as well as entertaining.

The theme for 1897, the sixtieth year of Her Majesty's reign, was easily decided. The Victorian Era Exhibition reviewed the period in all the obvious fields. Instead of a pageant, Sir Henry Irving and Sir Charles Wyndham took over Kiralfy's theatre to bring together the nation's leading dramatists and actors for the season. The exhibition opened to the biggest crowds ever seen at Earls Court. That afternoon Hartley and two constables went to the main entrance in Warwick Road (then, as now), to collate numbers from all the gates. As they neared the million mark Hartley closed the other entrances and kept only one turnstile working at Warwick Road until the millionth arrival clicked through – a fresh-faced young engine-driver. Hartley put a hand on his shoulder. His opening remark 'I want you' drew a shriek from his girlfriend – 'Bill, what have you done?' Explanations brought smiles and a handsome presentation watch, and a ludicrous warning from the Inland Revenue that the company had infringed the gambling laws.

Kiralfy's lavish productions appealed to national pride and routinely included the triumph of arms over lesser mortals. At Hartley's suggestion, 'Our Naval Victories' was

Captain Paul Boyton's water chute, 1899. He flooded the Earls Court arena in 1893 and built the 70ft-high chute backing on to Lillie Road at today's West Brompton entrance to Earls Court. *(GHL, The Graphic)*

staged there in 1898 as part of the International Universal Exhibition. Fleets of large model warships manoeuvred in the flooded arena. The programme ended with a noisy sea battle by night, a hidden man lying prone in each capital ship to control its movements, gunnery and torpedoes. Two unmanned ships struck mines, blew up and sank when small charges aboard were electrically detonated. Gun-flashes and explosions were realistically augmented by men concealed in the roof, cued to bomb vessels with sachets of sodium soaked in petrol which ignited violently in contact with water.

Tragically, a man was killed and two others severely injured when the unventilated magazine containing the explosives overheated in hot sunlight, self-igniting the explosives and blowing up at 5.10pm on 18 July. Mercifully, it happened between performances when few people were about. The nearby exhibition offices abutting the south end of the Theatre were wrecked and many houses lost their windows.

LCC inspectors had condemned the original cool underground store prepared by the company, insisting instead on a sheet-iron 'sentry box' structure above ground. This became a ready-primed bomb containing 40lb of gunpowder, tins of sodium and about 5 gallons of petrol in an open bath. The poor fellow who died on the spot was a 68-year-old Midland Railway employee who was sweeping an access ramp to the rail sheds nearby. A 12ft iron girder fell on the offices, the remains being set on fire by a sodium shower. Rushing back from the Western Gardens to find the offices ablaze, Hartley's first question to the dazed clerical staff outside was 'Have you got the books out?' The answer was 'No'. He called for assistance and bravely rescued them at the cost of his top hat and suit. Captain Wells, the company fire chief, was at his wits' end. There was sodium all over the place, exploding fiercely and burning whenever his men played their hoses on it. Loud explosions continued for two hours. Reports of 'Earls Court in Flames' brought people there in thousands. London Exhibitions cleared £14,000 on the 'Naval Victories' show alone.

The Military Exhibition of 1901 covered much more than the ongoing Boer War. Visitors were perhaps taken aback to find themselves confronted on arrival at the Warwick Road entrance not by some massive piece of ordnance but by a hand-operated hay press. The patent machine compacted loose hay into bales, saving much shipping capacity in the dispatch of fodder to the British Army's many thousands of horses and mules in South Africa.

In the Empress Theatre Kiralfy produced a dramatic account of the recent Boxer Rebellion and the relief of the legations in Peking, attended by much gunfire. On the lake a company of Royal Engineers built a pontoon bridge for a wagon column to cross, and by way of a complete change of scene, trips were offered 'down the Canton River' in boats that floated freely past 'highly realistic views of green rice fields with native coolies toiling in the plantations, and all the fascinating quaintness of China'. Captain Boyton's water chute had become one of London's popular pastimes. 'Shooting the chute' down the 350ft slide from a height of 70ft was claimed to be the biggest such ride on either side of the Atlantic. For the less adventurous there were always cruising motor launches, while the most thrilling act had to be the young American lady who, as 'The Living Shell', was fired twice-daily from a cannon directly into the car of a suspended balloon.

Visitors followed the progress of the Americas Cup yacht race via telegrams projected on to a large screen in the Queen's Court. As each arrived at the offices of the *Daily Graphic* it was read by telephone to the showground where messenger boys then rushed the text to the operator of a 'Lumiscriptor', by which means it reached the screen.

After Kiralfy's highly evocative Paris in London Exhibition in 1902, the last big Earls Court show in which he was to be fully engaged was the following year's International Fire Exhibition. Its success depended entirely on the Empress Theatre production – outdoor demonstrations of horse-drawn engines in action and competitions were not enough. Kiralfy had to stage a realistic spectacle in the arena, preferably something just short of burning down the theatre.

'Fighting the Flames' had a cast of 500 trained firemen and others. It opened with demonstrations of fire-fighting equipment and methods ranging from Roman soldiery with their squirts to the latest German techniques. The great stagefront along one side of the theatre was built up

The 'Red Dragon' train at Earls Court's Paris in London Exhibition, 1902. The narrow-gauge railway with its threepenny rides was a hardy annual. (*Arthur Smith collection*)

as a main thoroughfare of imposing four- and five-storey houses. A notice was walked across it asking the audience not to be alarmed when cries of 'Fire' were heard.

The theatre darkens. The scene is lit by street lamps. Amusing and typical events occur: a barmaid's walking race; a music hall empties, its audience boarding cabs and horse-buses. Suddenly there is a distant 'thump' and light-play behind the blinds on an upper floor. A serious lamp explosion in a workroom! Cries of 'Fire! Fire!' Shadows of people rushing about the room. Soon the street door flies open as numbers flee, a blazing staircase visible behind them as burning oil flows down, trapping others on upper floors. A passing cart pulls up against the wall and rescues victims from lower windows. A policeman arrives and runs to an alarm post.

Partly clad residents flee adjoining buildings as the local fire brigade's hand escape, hose cart and four firemen arrive. They call for reinforcements. A jumping-sheet catches two unfortunates from a second-storey window. Three victims get on to the roof and are rescued by a horse escape team which has dashed to the scene. The first steamer arrives; its superintendent's commands bring order and soon jets are playing through the windows. More steamers gallop in. Hoses are run out and huge quantities

of water are now directed on to the conflagration as further escapes complete the rescues. The flames rise higher. Suddenly a woman and child appear on the fiercely burning top floor. She rushes from window to window screaming for help. The street crowd breaks through the police cordon. The audience is enthralled, groaning and shouting helpful advice to her: 'Go back!' 'Stay there!' 'Get on the roof!' Cheers attend a fireman's brave rescue attempt through smoke and flame up an outsize ladder – the poor woman is finally across his shoulder, still clutching her child, just as the roof collapses and takes the floors with it. As they reach the ground, deafening cheers rise from all parts of the house. Some 1,500 gallons of water per minute soon deadens the blaze, conveniently draining into the pool. The enormous safety curtain falls to prolonged cheering.

Behind the scenes hidden actors in heavy flannel overalls tended the fires to electric signal cues, dodging the great heat and inrush of water. The women courageously entered burning rooms to be 'rescued'. The team was nicknamed 'The Water-Dodgers' Brigade'.

An Italian Exhibition with 'Venice by Night' followed in 1904. The Russian authorities approached the London Chamber of Commerce with a view to a Russian exhibition the year after. Harold Hartley went to St Petersburg to meet Foreign Minister Isvolsky and terms were agreed for an Earls Court show. The Russian government was to build and install the exhibition, but later inexplicably withdrew on advice from its London Embassy. Instead, Earls Court mounted a Naval, Shipping and Fisheries Exhibition in 1905 to mark the centenary of the Battle of Trafalgar. Visitors could take a trip in a submarine on the Queen's Court lake, or watch divers at work in a tank installed by Siebe Gorman. The theatre presented life aboard a cruiser in *With the Fleet*. Rather surprisingly a Red Indian village lay beside the lake, its braves in war canoes hardly reflecting the general maritime theme.

The Imperial Austrian Exhibition of 1906 was financially the most successful of the series. In place of the traditional Kiralfy spectacular, however, the theatre became a Tyrolean village. Kiralfy was disengaging from activities at Earls Court. He resigned as director-general at the close of the exhibition to prepare for what he later said was the summit of his life's achievements – the huge Franco-British Exhibition of 1908 at Shepherds Bush. Kiralfy built the great White City for it and had the added pleasure of working alongside his sons: Charles as general manager, Albert as director of works and Gerald as superintending architect. Harold Hartley's colleague Herman Hart took over from the great showman at Earls Court.

The Hungarian Exhibition in 1908 was notable for drawing 1.3 million visitors, peaking at over 50,000 on the day the Suffragette Movement staged a rally there. Hartley, a firm supporter of the movement, suggested the gathering which brought processions of members in their thousands from points across London. Mrs Pankhurst and other leaders of the movement later took tea with Mr and Mrs Hartley in the Old Welcome Club.

Kiralfy's colossal White City event that year was an early warning of trouble ahead from Shepherds Bush. Earls Court countered by putting down a large roller-skating and dance floor in the Empress Theatre for the winter season. The Golden West and

Strolling among the many amusements and shops at Earls Court's Italian Exhibition, 1904. (H&FA)

American Industries Exhibition of 1909 attempted to resurrect Buffalo Bill without Cody – but it was *Hamlet* without the prince. The following year London Exhibitions Ltd paid off its debentures, handed over its assets to the creditors and assigned its leases and agreements to a new company, Earls Court Ltd. No event was staged in 1910.

The showgrounds fell into decline. Four or five events were staged before war closed them. One is noteworthy for its pedigree and technical excellence even though it was a financial disaster. 'Shakespeare's England' in 1912 was promoted and organised by Mrs George Cornwallis West (Lady Randolph Churchill). She booked the Empress Hall for a production which ranged from jousting to jesters and Morris dancing to glee singers. On stage a superbly realistic group of ancient houses and taverns adjoined the Globe Theatre. The famous Eglinton Tournament of 1839 was re-created in the arena. The original had been an aristocratic and, as it turned out, wet-weather romp with horses and armour on the lawns of Eglinton Castle in Ayrshire. The Earls Court version's aristocratic cast of knights and their ladies included Viscountess Curzon as 'The Queen of Beauty' with the Duke of Marlborough and six Lords, all in armour, together with their squires, gonfalons, bowmen and servants.

The Lillie Road entrance to the Imperial Royal Austrian Exhibition, Earls Court, 1906. The Gigantic Wheel can just be seen in the distance behind the right-hand flagpole. *(H&FA)*

King Edward VII visits the Austrian Exhibition in 1906. On his left, with cane, is Count Mensdorff-Pouilly-Dietrichstein, Austro-Hungarian Ambassador. *(Arthur Smith collection)*

Sir Hiram Maxim's captive airships, Balkan States Exhibition, Earls Court, 1907. *(H&FA)*

Ready for a 'Joy Wheel'
ride during the
'Shakespeare's England'
exhibition, Earls Court,
1912. (H&FA)

The show ran at a loss for a month or two before Charles Cochran's services were requested by its guarantors to get it back on an even keel. There were disagreements, principally over Lady Randolph's stage directions. Cockie introduced a good circus, there being no obvious alternative at the height of the season, but it was too late to recover all the earlier losses.

The masters

Kiralfy wrote later:

It is very gratifying to me to think that I have never rested content with that which both my friends and critics have thought to be my best. I fear I have never followed the adage and let well enough alone. Still more gratifying is the thought that I may have helped to raise the standard of spectacular entertainment and that I have contributed something to the artistic needs as well as to the gaiety of nations.

He became a British subject in 1901, living at the Tower House in Cromwell Road, London. He died of a heart attack in Brighton on 27 April 1919. Kiralfy had determined to build on Whitley's pioneering start, to create a handsome and more durable showground which would amaze, delight and inform millions with the scale, creativity and sheer fun of his productions. He achieved all these things and for twelve years he reigned triumphantly .

John Whitley, Imre Kiralfy and Harold Hartley *were* the Golden Age of Earls Court.

SIX
OLYMPIA
The Lotus Years

'To appear at Olympia was to put the cachet on a reputation, or even to make one. There is barely an artiste of international repute who has not appeared there.'

Frank Foster, equestrian director and ringmaster,
Bertram Mills' Circus, undated memoir

THE BELGIAN GOVERNMENT received an ultimatum from Germany on 2 August 1914 demanding free passage for her troops. When the Belgians refused to allow their neutrality to be violated, the Germans marched in two days later. A British ultimatum to Germany that same day was ignored by Berlin, and the country was at war. Olympia was requisitioned as a temporary civil prison camp for German nationals and other potentially hostile aliens. From 1915 the hall spent the rest of the war as an army clothing store.

Zeppelin airships began to raid southern England in January 1915, alarming London and causing property values to fall. Sir Gilbert Greenall took advantage of this to buy up West Kensington Gardens which lay between Olympia and Hammersmith Road, gaining rental income from the properties and a future opportunity to expand. It is unclear whether the purchase included the adjoining bank and the Bell and Anchor pub on the corner of Blythe Road (both since demolished and their site covered by Olympia 2 car park).

Olympia was derequisitioned in 1919, its first letting going to Charles Cochran's heavyweight fight promotion between Joe Beckett and Frank Goddard on 17 June. Goddard, the 6ft 3in tall ex-Guardsman, was knocked out in the second round. Olympia's release had been a close-run thing. The War Office had adamantly refused to vacate the hall when approached in January by the organisers of the Tournament, who then insisted on having confirmation in writing. That did the trick and the Army moved out. The newly renamed Royal Naval, Military and Air Force Tournament returned in June, its cumbersome title being shortened to the Royal Tournament the following year. Industry was still struggling to change back to peacetime production and few exhibitions had restarted. The Motor Show returned to gladden hearts that November. It was an impossible squeeze and for the next three years the overspill was housed at Kiralfy's White City, linked by a bus shuttle.

What became Olympia's traditional Christmas Circus had begun with Hagenbeck's long run in 1913/14. It was now resumed for shorter winter seasons, starting with Fred

White's British Amusements at Bertram Mills' Circus, Olympia, 1924/5. The Big Top is visible beyond. Photography was not up to handling moving crowds so most of Olympia's early images were taken in an empty hall. Note the high-diver's ladder and pool at left. *(ECO)*

Wilkins' Great Royal Victory Circus and Fun Fair in 1919/20. Bertram Mills' Circus and Fun Fair followed in succeeding years, becoming a much-loved event for three generations of young and young at heart until 1965. Mills made Olympia a name to aspire to in the circus world – and it all began by accident.

Bertram Wagstaff Mills (1873–1938), a successful pre-war coach builder by trade and now a newly demobilised RASC captain, had always loved horses. This led to a friendship with Reginald Heaton, Olympia's managing director and founder of its Horse Show. After watching Fred Wilkins' rather uninspiring circus the two discussed it over supper. Knowing Mills' abilities, Heaton persuaded the inexperienced captain to fulfil his own assertion that he could have done better. Mills took a tenancy for the following Christmas and booked John Ringling's Barnum & Bailey Circus from the USA, the world's largest. Ringling had to cancel in June because of lack of shipping. Mills could have asked Heaton to release him from the tenancy, but instead he toured Europe picking up acts with Cyril, his eighteen-year-old son. Full dress rehearsal on the day before opening was nightmarish. It overran the two-and-a-half hour programme by more than two hours. Bertram spent the rest of the night with the ringmaster shortening and rescheduling acts. The show was a triumph of enthusiasm over ignorance.

Mills shared Cochran's gift for promotion. His graphics expert Leon Crossley, who worked with him for forty years from 1924 onwards, would study rehearsals before producing memorable publicity. London hoardings in December 1925 carried 'teaser'

L.R. Brightwell's 'Now the Pie is Open' poster artwork for Bertram Mills Olympia Circus, 1929/30. The pencilled text beneath reads: 'It must be a jaded palate that cannot enjoy the tasty dish Mr Bertram Mills has concocted at Olympia. There is something to suit all tastes. The artistic is happily blended with the humorous, for the ingredients include equestrian turns, acrobatics, amazing elephant act … impossible … birds, and a liberal seasoning of clown sauce. In the last, Whimsical Walker, the clown who is not too old at seventy odd, figures very prominently. This year marks the "pie's" first decade – and like vintage port and Walker the Whimsical – it improves with every year.'
(K. Whitehouse collection)

posters simply announcing 'LOOK OUT, 70 ARE COMING'. A fortnight later 'TO OLYMPIA' was added. All was revealed when seventy lions were driven through London in a convoy of circus wagons carrying huge posters reading '70 LIONS GOING TO OLYMPIA'. In reply to a parliamentary question the Home Office boosted ticket sales after confirming that it was unable to prevent such a dangerous performance in the ring. A Bengal tiger was born in the hall in 1933. A year or so later Rudolph Matthies the trainer was to be seen walking it through the streets and declaring it to be Olympia's own tiger.

The circus world was a closed community of families with its own traditions, hierarchy and evocative smells. Here is how *The Times* described its mystique in 1927:

King George VI, Queen Elizabeth and the young princesses visit Bertram Mills' Christmas Circus at Olympia. (ECO)

> You enter Olympia; you smell from afar the tan, the horses and the elephants; you go to your seat beneath a roof blazing with lights and dripping with trapezes; you hear approaching the harsh voices of Whimsical Walker and his fellow clowns. Instantly the spell descends. A circus is much more than an aggregate of turns. It has a genial collective spirit.

As with any circus, there were occasional misjudgements and accidents at Olympia. At Christmas 1927 there was an act in which a horse and girl rider were hoisted into the air on a platform with ample safety rails. Astonishingly, fireworks were then exploded. As the smoke cleared it could be seen that one of the horse's legs had slipped from the platform. It was never in danger of falling, but horse and audience were clearly unhappy as the rig was carefully lowered to the ground. The act was not suited to an English ring. What the rest of it entailed is unknown. On another occasion three elephants en route to the ring in 1954 were frightened by a stallholder's Pomeranian dog. They lumbered into a sideshow and brought it crashing down on a midget couple. The 2ft 6in tall husband was unharmed but his 4ft wife suffered two broken ribs. The elephants went steadily on to perform.

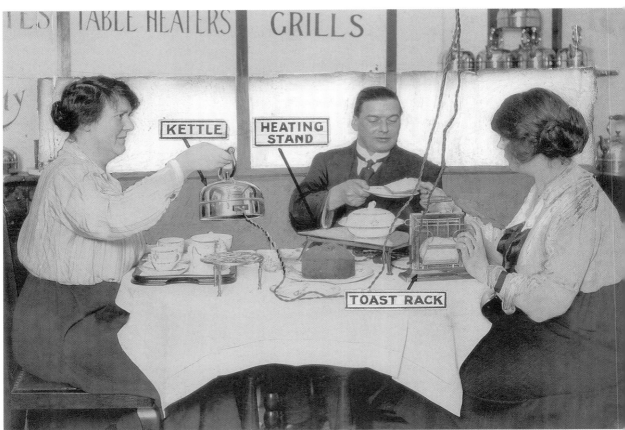

A tragic fatality followed the fall of 'wall of death' motorcyclist Arno Wickbold. He performed in a metal lattice cage 65ft above the ring, the base of the cage being opened at a given point leaving only a safety net beneath him. On the evening of 27 December 1951 Wickbold's engine cut out and he and the bike fell to the ground, narrowly missing the net. He died three days later.

Looking ahead at 'Ideal Homes'

The Ideal Home Exhibition returned in 1920 with a topical competition for Ideal (Workers') Homes. It reflected the theme of the 1919 Housing Act which promised 'homes fit for heroes' for returning soldiers, and by implication for all those engaged on the Home Front in war production. Domestic hygiene and labour-saving features were key requirements and were reflected in displays throughout the show.

The war freed women in many ways. Suffrage had been granted to those aged over thirty who were householders or the wife of a householder, and women now enjoyed legal and political rights. They could freely pursue careers hitherto closed to them by regulation or tradition. The role of the housewife subtly changed too, declining for many from chatelaine to housekeeper, and from housekeeper to 'domestic'. Servants were scarce and expensive. Women were increasingly concerned with household management and efficiency. The show gave them both.

Lord Northcliffe promoted a national efficiency drive in 1921. The Ideal Home Exhibition was replaced for that year only by the *Daily Mail* Efficiency Exhibition. It included the workplace and highlighted the rehabilitation and training of disabled ex-servicemen. The whole of the Annexe was fitted up as workshops in which the men demonstrated their skills at forty different trades, even including the production of artificial limbs. In 1934, in the deepening depression, an element of self-mockery crept into the exhibition. The more exotic labour-saving devices were becoming ridiculed as 'gadgets'. W. Heath Robinson, the cartoonist and manic genius of mechanical mis-improvisation, presented a crazy appliance-filled house, called 'The Gadgets'. The walls of the 20ft-high building were cut away to reveal various rooms in which the animated Glowmutton family were preoccupied with wildly improbable domestic equipment in action, as also in the garden.

In 1936 a large 'House of the Future' exhibit was based on the forecasts of H.G. Wells who predicted no corners, pillars or windows. Other innovations included animated images as wall decoration so that clouds, landscapes or flowers drifted tranquilly across the plain surface. The sun's rays were captured and diffused throughout the air-conditioned house at all hours. Push-button meals were automatically prepared and delivered by conveyor. The 1937 'All-In Home' show house went one further and dispensed with internal walls. Instead, mobile storage units doubled as room dividers to allow major changes in layout while removing all need for fitted cupboards.

Tea dances and tragedies

Back in July 1920, Olympia's International Aero Exhibition proved surprisingly disappointing, the public showing little interest. Bombers had been refitted for civil use and the Air Ministry demonstrated the many technical and safety advances arising from combat experience, but the air war was too painful a memory. The aviation industry returned only once to Olympia, in 1929.

The Motor Show's pressing need for more space was met by a decision to demolish the four most easterly houses in West Kensington Gardens together with the remaining Vineyard Nursery buildings fronting Addison Road, to make way for another hall. James Carmichael of Wandsworth was contracted on 23 April 1922 to build 'New Hall' for £494,000. It is a smaller and lower version of the main hall but it increased Olympia's exhibition space by over 9,000 sq. metres to 28,000 sq. metres in all. Architect Joseph Emberton chose an unadorned external style. The completed hall was first let for a tobacco exhibition in May 1923. This worried Bertram Mills who was determined to block any chance of a competing event getting the hall during his circus tenancy. He booked New Hall himself, incidentally gaining valuable advertising space along its Hammersmith Road frontage. Mills put down 7,000 sq. metres of dance floor, expecting a high-class turnout. He got it – but drunks and layabouts followed them in off the street. Circus attendants were hastily drafted across and given handfuls of half-crowns to encourage the intruders to go away and find a pub.

Thereafter the public flocked to 'The World's Greatest Dance-Hall'. Regular attendances approaching 4,000 at a time waltzed and fox-trotted under thousands of balloons on 30 miles of Japanese oak strip floor, its glassy panels maintained by a motorised glazing machine. Musical director George Burrows was a stickler for decorous enjoyment to the highest standards: no lady could wear a hat save at

Some exhibits at early motor shows arrived on the back of a cart. Display cars were frequently over-prepared, many chassis polished to a mirror finish. Driving them to the hall was undesirable. This is Olympia in 1924. *(H&FA)*

Foundation trenches of the New Hall, viewed from Hammersmith Road, 25 June 1922. The first show opened there in May 1923. *(ECO)*

BRITISH QUAIN SUNLIGHT Ltd.
20/21. LAURENCE POUNTNEY LANE, CANNON ST E.C.4.

Over-heated sleeper ringed by fires – the one in the bathroom looks especially lethal. Building Exhibition, Olympia, 1936. *(Montgomery Exhibitions)*

afternoon Tea Dances; no 'spinning, shimmying or grotesque steps' were permitted; no smoking was allowed on the floor; and dancers had to keep moving round. The blues were treated with caution. Initial acoustic problems were overcome after experts advised a lattice of suspended chicken wire and sound relays – hence the balloon camouflage. New Hall remained a public ballroom until February 1925, breaking off only for the Ideal Home and Building Exhibitions. The floor was re-laid for each circus until 1928.

For two consecutive seasons after the war the Royal Tournament's 1st Air Defence Brigade made the rather alarming discovery of a Zeppelin in the roof – and shot it down twice-daily. The 1919 programme included a satisfyingly noisy demonstration by a MkV 2-star tank operating self-bridging equipment under fire; a competition between women motor drivers, not forgetting wheel changing and reversing through gateways – points were deducted for erratic driving; and a striking display of physical training by a hundred airmen swinging illuminated Indian clubs in the darkened arena. The General Strike of May 1926 forced postponement of the Tournament to July. As with the circus, the most dangerous stunts cost lives. A Royal Horse Artillery driver died during a practice musical ride at Albany Barracks in 1925 when a gun cornering at speed rolled over. A naval stoker lost his life practising at Portsmouth in 1937 for the field gun competition.

Catering for all tastes

By the late 1920s Olympia had built a firm base of annual 'regulars' in its exhibitions calendar. Aside from those previously mentioned, additions embraced machine tools, shipping engineering and marine, furniture trades and printing, advertising and marketing, cookery and food, holidays and travel, fashions and hairdressing exhibitions.

Joe Lyons, the official caterer, regularly produced luncheons and dinners for thousands but the 'Feast of the 8,000' in 1925 remained in the folk memory at Olympia for decades as the peak of organisational perfection. The occasion was a Masonic war memorial fund-raising dinner that August. The diners came from all over the world, paying 17 guineas a head. They sat at 3 miles of tables served by 1,360 waitresses (Lyons 'nippies'), supported by 700 cooks and porters with 86,000 glasses and plates in use – breakages totalled 3,500. To calm the nerves of this vast army Lyons screened a comedy film before the function, ending with the message 'We've done our best – now it's up to you. Good luck!' Their 'field-marshal' sat in a room with earphones, a console and a clock. Every movement of every nippie was pre-plotted and all commands were by buzzer. The great hall with its thousand white-shrouded

Weighty matters at the Royal Tournament soon after the First World War. This 35-ton MkV 2-star tank would have chewed up Olympia's floor, making lots of noise in the process. All crews carried side arms to repel boarders. The notice strictly prohibits smoking. *(AC)*

tables set with shining glass and silver, red menus upright among them, looked like a huge snowfield scattered with crimson poppies. The magic, and perhaps the unintended symbolism, stayed in the minds of all there that day.

The National Wireless & Radio Exhibition transferred to Olympia from the Albert Hall in 1926. Attendance leapt that year from 54,500 visitors to 116,570 in its new home. It continued until 1939 when the war stopped play. This immensely popular show – renamed 'Radiolympia' in 1936 – returned to the hall after the war but left in 1950 because a change of dates could not be secured. In 1931 it claimed to be the world's largest radio exhibition. By then primitive acid battery 'cat's whisker' sets had long been overtaken by pocket-size radios right up to 12ft-high radio-gramophones or 'radiograms'. 'Alpha' the Robot arrived the following year complete with photo-electric cells behind his eye gratings, and his ears concealing microphones. His life-like metal body moved its limbs, stood and sat to voice commands, and he answered simple questions. To general amazement the show had been opened from Ottawa, 4,000 miles distant, via trans-Atlantic 'beam wireless'. The BBC took space for the first time in 1933 when over 225,000 attended.

Radiolympia captivated a public hungry for the magic of the wireless set. Mullard Valves trained these demonstrators for its 1929 display. *(ECO)*

Growth, and the gathering storm

After a clear run of seventeen years Olympia changed hands again in 1929. Olympia (1912) Ltd was bought for £1 million by Philip Ernest Hill, chairman of Covent Garden Properties Ltd. He formed Olympia Ltd, announcing the purchase on 27 February and taking possession on 25 March. The long-serving Reginald Heaton continued as managing director. With amazing luck Hill saw the biggest exhibition fish in the country jump into his net only days after buying Olympia. He never had to cast a fly over the London section of the British Industries Fair (BIF) which had occupied Kiralfy's White City since 1921. That year's BIF closed just before Hill's deal went public. It had been fogged in for the entire period and the exhibitors complained bitterly about the cold and inadequate halls and demanded a move to Olympia. The Fair's sponsors, the Department of Overseas Trade's Empire Marketing Board, quickly booked into Olympia from 1930 for ten years. Had Sir Gilbert Greenall been given the slightest expectation of securing the BIF then his price for Olympia would have been much higher.

Opposite, above: 8,000 for dinner! The Royal Masonic Festival dines in Grand Hall, 1925. *(ECO)*

Below: The cathedral-like setting for Radiolympia – Grand Hall, 1933. *(ECO)*

Having caged the beast, Hill knew that if he was to keep it he had to find it more space. The 1,500 display stands with a combined frontage of 6 miles were still growing. He built the four-storey Empire Hall (now Olympia 2) in line with the New Hall fronting Hammersmith Road. It was erected primarily for the BIF, as its name confirms. The new hall displaced the remaining four West Kensington Gardens properties but left standing No. 34, a bank, and the Bell and Anchor pub, both fronting Hammersmith Road. Behind them, two blocks of flats comprising Addison Court Gardens also survived. These all occupied the site of the present Olympia 2 car park. The bank and pub were demolished around 1967/8, and Addison Court almost certainly went ten years earlier.

The Empire Hall was also built to Joseph Emberton's design, adding 20,000 sq. metres to Olympia's letting capacity which now totalled nearly 50,000 sq. metres. Space limitations at ground level meant the multi-floor building was configured much like a department store (Emberton later designed Simpson's in Piccadilly). Remarkably it opened on time for the BIF in February 1930 at a cost of £580,000. Emberton's adjoining New Hall was renamed the National Hall, and the main building became the Grand Hall. A covered footbridge was built across Addison Road to link the station directly with the Grand Hall.

Visitors to the 1929 Motor Show were plagued by legions of pushy salesmen. The SMMT clamped down, badging bona fide reps and limiting the numbers on each stand. As for the cars, fabric-covered coachwork remained popular at the upper end of the market in preference to metal bodies and cellulose finishes. Running boards were on the way out and lockable doors were coming in. Luggage was almost invariably still perched on a hinged grid at the rear in a 'motor trunk'. Light 8hp and 12hp saloon cars

were best sellers; 37,000 were registered between March and July that year. Interest in sports cars leapt three years later with the launch at Olympia of the MG Magnette, including a 'blown' version capable of 130mph. Motoring taxes remained a thorny subject, then as now. The SMMT claimed that British owners were paying on average £28 per year in tax, almost twice the burden of any other country.

Wheels of another kind came to Olympia in 1934, introducing British audiences to a sport with a fanatical following abroad. The United Kingdom's first International Six-Day Cycle Team Race was staged on a boarded track banked to allow speeds of up to 100mph. Its construction required 5 tons of nails. The 142-hour competition between fifteen teams was more than a gut-busting endurance battle – tactics were varied and complex, sometimes enabling teams to gain a full lap. Enthusiasts went in satisfying numbers but the sport never really caught on nationally.

The voracious demands of the BIF for more space gave Hill no rest. His Empire Hall satisfied it for just one year. In 1931 it had again outgrown Olympia and a section was forced to return to the White City. Hill announced in February 1933 that he would build a colossal hall less than 150yd south-east of Olympia on the corner of Kensington High Street and Warwick Road, where Charles House stands today. (Olympia's land bank of 1895 was long gone.) Joseph Emberton prepared outline plans for a handsome structure with 45,000 sq. metres of exhibition space on the 3.5-acre site, almost doubling Olympia's capacity. Its main roof clear-spanned 245ft, the widest in Europe and probably the world. The hall would be connected to Olympia by a subway. A new station would adjoin the bridge there to serve both centres. Philip Hill put in a planning application to the LCC, after which the project quietly died. Over the next eighteen months it became clear that the BIF had its own quite different ideas for its future accommodation. Olympia was not part of them.

Hill would construct one more major facility at Olympia – London's first multi-storey car park. It stands on the Maclise Road frontage and is to Joseph Emberton's design. It opened in 1937.

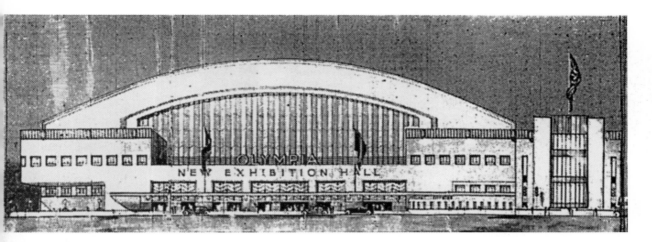

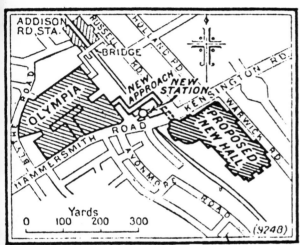

Olympia announced plans in 1933 for a colossal new hall across Hammersmith Road where Charles House now stands. A railway station would be built between the two halls with dedicated access to each. Olympia's giant British Industries Fair had other ideas and today's Earls Court was built specifically for it, sinking Philip Hill's scheme. *(ECO)*

The Women's League of Health & Beauty, Olympia, 1936. *(ECO)*

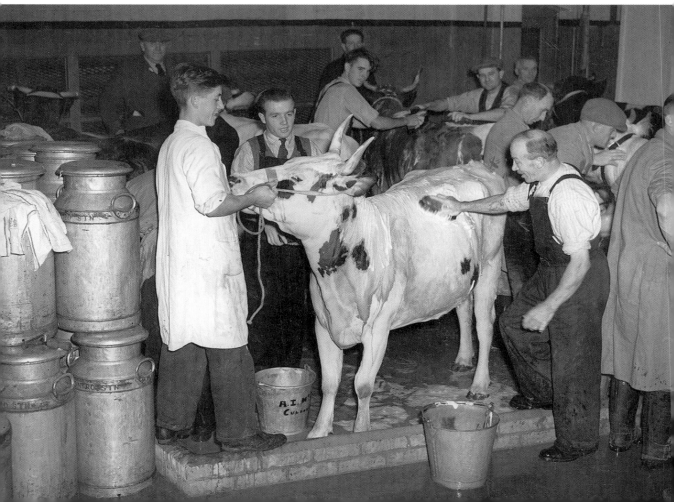

In the same week in 1933 that Hill announced his great scheme, the flames of the burning Reichstag lit Berlin's night sky. On 7 June the following year the blackshirt rally of Sir Oswald Mosley's British Union of Fascists filled Grand Hall. The meeting had been heavily infiltrated by left-wingers bent on trouble. Their orchestrated interruptions were met with savage beatings from the stewards before the objectors were thrown out into the street. One man climbed the iron trusses into the roof and sat there catcalling, breaking through the high glass and escaping as his pursuers came near. Mosley did nothing from the podium to dampen down the situation, which ended in near chaos.

Olympia's lotus years were fading as another war threatened.

Above: The uncrowned King Edward VIII departs from the Building Exhibition with founder Greville Montgomery on his right, Olympia, 1936. *(Montgomery Exhibitions)*

Opposite, left: Olympia's International Pro Tennis Tournament in 1939.
Left to right: Ramillon (France), Nusslein the singles winner (Germany), Palmieri (Italy), Kozeluh (Czechoslovakia), Stoeffen and Tilden (USA). *(ECO)*

Right: Olympia's imaginative racquet-shaped dinner table salute to the Tennis Tournament in 1939. *(ECO)*

Below: Final grooming, Olympia Dairy Show, 1937. *(ECO)*

SEVEN

EARLS COURT
Phoenix – and Ashes

'The future of Earls Court lies as much in the realm of spectacular entertainment as of exhibition production. The trend of public demand today is toward large-scale spectacle and sensation.'

Robert J. Siddall, consulting engineer to the Earls Court project,
The Engineer, 31 December 1937

LONG AFTER THE EVENT, an elderly lady recalled in a Fulham newspaper that a German orchestra was playing in the old Earls Court showgrounds late one summer evening in 1914. Abruptly the music stopped, the musicians quietly gathered up their instruments and departed. An English band took their seats and at once played the National Anthem. As of 11pm that evening, 4 August, Britain and Germany were at war.

Earls Court Ltd surrendered its lease on the site and went into liquidation. The lease was taken up by the hastily formed Earls Court Grounds Ltd (ECG). Its chairman Murray Griffith was briefly joined on the board by Pa Payne, late of Olympia, but he resigned the following May. The Empress Theatre and grounds were requisitioned on 13 October by the Local Government Board as a reception and processing centre, primarily for Belgian refugees. The Sunny Spain Exhibition which was still running for those with any stomach for holiday planning, closed that afternoon. Two days later 1,387 refugees arrived. The little children among them were thrilled next morning to find a large menagerie in the old ballroom, awaiting transport out.

The centre became a well-run camp housing up to 2,000 refugees at a time. Its director Mr G.A. Powell opened workshops there in November 1915 for military clothing contracts. Later, a large unit turned out ammunition boxes. The palatial but run-down buildings were adapted, with linoleum floor-covering serving as room dividers. The Queen's Palace on the triangle became a married quarters, and the Empress Theatre a dining hall and dormitory. *The Times* considered it all a 'quasi-Utopia'.

The centre closed and departed in July 1919. The Queen's Palace and surrounding area were taken by the London General Omnibus Company at £800 per annum as a depot for unwanted buses. It later put in a bid (unsuccessfully) for the whole site. Occasional circuses and fairs came and went. The Theatre became a store and workshop. Hoardings concealed the ruinous gardens and decaying buildings. In 1929 the Underground Electric Railways Company sought a partner to erect 'a very large

building' on the site. There were no takers. ECG surrendered the lease in 1934 and a receiver moved in.

The breakthrough came a year later. The pressing question of providing adequate accommodation for the British Industries Fair had been raised in Parliament. It was proposed that the government should take the initiative and build an exhibition centre specifically for the BIF. The idea was refused because it would be insanely wasteful to have such a building standing empty for nearly eleven months each year. (This is exactly what happened in Germany after the Second World War. Nuremberg's big new state and regionally funded hall was one of several which housed only one fair each year, albeit a leading European event. Exhibitors' stands could remain permanently *in situ*). It was pointed out that the hall could be let for other exhibitions for the rest of the year, but this too was unacceptable as it would place the government in competition with private operators in a highly speculative market.

Earls Court was a refugee centre throughout the First World War. It was an open camp for Belgians at first, then for escaping allied prisoners and refugees from Russia and Serbia. This was the women's clothing store. All clothing for the camp was made on site. *(H&FA)*

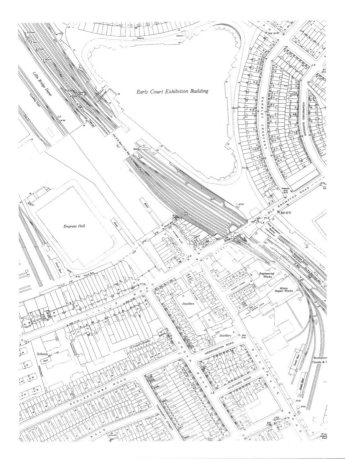

Earls Court between 1937 and 1960 before Empress Hall was demolished. Note Brompton goods yard, bottom right, once the Lillie Bridge Athletic Ground and now Earls Court's main car park. *(Crown copyright, Ordnance Survey, 1950)*

Carmen at Earls Court, 1989. This enormous stage is being built over the emptied 4m deep pool to allow for under-floor access and special effects. Such versatility on this scale is unique to Earls Court. *(ECO)*

Sick of the political pussyfooting, a group of industrialists responded in 1935 with their own proposals for a new exhibition and event centre at Earls Court to house the entire BIF in a world-class facility. Earls Court Ltd was at once formed under the chairmanship of Sir Ralph Glyn, a director of the LMS Railway Company and chairman of the British Pacific Trust. He was joined by Mr Frank R. Lewis, a dynamic exhibition and event organiser, as managing director. The new company secured substantial American backing through Glyn's Trust.

The freehold of the old showground had passed to the London Passenger Transport Board. Glyn secured a 99-year lease on the 12-acre Kensington triangle and a further 6 acres on the other side of the railway, which included the Empress Theatre. He already had assurances that the BIF would move in on completion, and now signed up the Ideal Home and Motor Shows before spreading the net wider.

Superb as accessibility was in the triangle, with underground stations opposite the front and back gates, the problem remained that it was crossed by four separate sets of railway tracks, two double and two single lines. They branched out of Earls Court station to run through the site in open cuttings or tunnels to join the West London Extension Railway lines across its rear. On these fragmented 12 acres a giant steel and concrete building was to be erected, covering 9 of them. Its 'footprint' was more than twice that of St Paul's Cathedral. The roof would entirely cover Trafalgar Square.

Earls Court was never intended simply to compete with Olympia. It was planned to dominate what its management and workpeople called 'the village hall' up the road, just as Olympia's build strategy had been directed against the Aggie fifty years before. Glyn laid down his basic requirements.

Frank R. Lewis, sports promoter, joined the board as MD of Earls Court Ltd on its formation in 1935. He was chairman 1965–8, then president until 1972 when Sterling Guarantee acquired the hall. (ECO)

- The building must provide a total of 42,000 sq. metres of exhibition floor space on not more than two levels.
- Seating for 23,000 in a column-free auditorium overlooking an arena, in the middle of which must be a giant pool.
- The entire auditorium including the pool and seating to be convertible at speed to flat-floor exhibition space.
- Parking on site for 2,000 cars.

The hall's ability to provide large-scale spectator events under cover was as important as housing the BIF. It would have been a testing specification on a greenfield site, but for a rail-slashed triangular parcel of unstable ground it was awesome. No other show centre in the world then or since has required so much to be compressed into so little on so misshapen a site.

The very experienced US firm of Hegeman-Harris Co. Inc. was appointed as lead contractor, having filled this position for New York's Rockefeller Centre. The Earls

Within the photograph:
Earls Court Exhibition B
Progress Photo Date 29·
HEGEMAN HARRIS CO. Inc.
View from Motorpool

Earls Court 1, Warwick Road frontage, December 1936. Note the horse-drawn wagons. *(ECO)*

Court contract stipulated that only British sub-contractors and labour should be employed, and British materials used wherever possible.

Hegeman-Harris engaged an eminent American architect, Mr Charles Howard Crane (1885–1952) of Detroit. He specialised in the design of large entertainment centres, the apex of his career probably being the city's Fox Theatre which opened in 1928 and stands today as one of his major achievements. It seated over 5,000 people and had design features in amazing proportions. The otherwise plain external lines of Crane's London hall are enlivened by small touches of Art Deco in the detailing. Richard Tames notes in his *Earls Court and Brompton Past* that Crane's Warwick Road façade strongly resembles an unbuilt design for an International Music Hall and Opera House intended for Hyde Park Corner, produced by a consortium of which Crane was a member in the 1930s. The 3,000-seat Gaumont Holloway cinema in Islington is his work, built in 1938. Crane remained in England throughout the war designing armament works and is credited with helping to rebuild London afterwards.

Howard Crane produced 1,270 drawings for Earls Court's builders. The structure would be Europe's biggest by volume and was believed to be the largest area in the

End-game, March/April 1939. The swastika flag marked Germany's participation – and victory – in the men's singles. *(ECO)*

National Radio Show, Earls Court, 1953. *(ECO)*

One of Claude Langdon's ice specials, Empress Hall, 1950. *(ECO)*

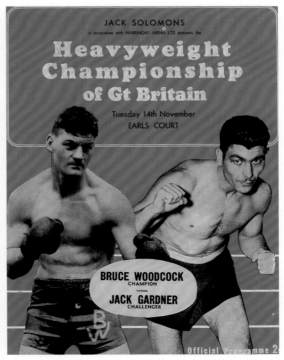

Woodcock vs Gardner at Earls Court, 1950. Woodcock retired after the 11th round. *(ECO)*

Hotelympia, 1984. *(ECO)*

Joe Bugner, Britain's European heavyweight champion, fights Joe Frazier of the US before a crowd of 15,000, Earls Court, 1973. Bugner narrowly lost on points. *(ECO)*

Elton John at Earls Court, 1993. *(ECO)*

Olympia International Showjumping Championships, 1982. *(ECO)*

Judging at Royal Smithfield, Earls Court, 1998.

Right: Glittering prizes.

Below: Networking. The Queen Mother, Smithfield, 1998.
(all Clarion Events)

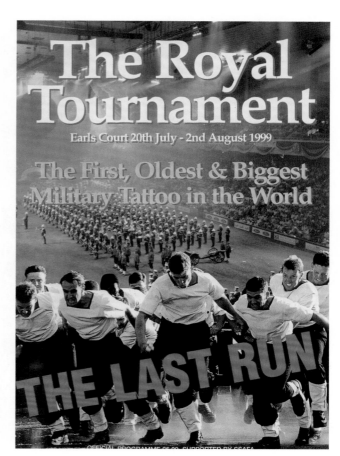

First to last – The Royal Tournament's years at Olympia and Earls Court, 1906–99. *(all ECO)*

Detail, cast-iron balustrade, Olympia, 1886. *(ECO)*

15 men, 10,000 litres of paint, 42 days – Olympia, 1988. *(ECO)*

Joseph Emberton's National Hall at Olympia, opened in 1923. *(ECO)*

Emberton built the handsome Apex Suite in 1922/23. *(ECO)*

Opposite, top: The Riyadh Exhibition, Olympia, 1986.
(ECO)

Right: Hotelympia, 1982. *(ECO)*

Attendances at Torvill and Dean's seventeen performances averaged 10,000 at Earls Court in 1990. *(ECO)*

Cruft's Dog Show came to Olympia in 1948, moving to Earls Court in 1979. This was the arena in 1983. *(ECO)*

Behind the scenes – rigging a ghostly battle squadron and laying soil in the arena for the Royal Tournament, Earls Court, 1993. *(ECO)*

world under one roof, with a clear span of 250ft. It was one of the first (and certainly the largest) of a new generation of concrete structures employing a steel-reinforced hollow-beam system. The building consumed 90,000 cu. yd of concrete, its 1,000-odd supporting columns carrying loads of up to 2,500 tons each. Many columns were directly over the rail tracks and these had to rest on massive portals or bridges. All supports were bedded on concrete foundation slabs. The alternative was to deep pile to 50ft, but this option was dismissed as the vibration risked bringing down the rail tunnels. The main exhibition floor had to be suspended 15ft above ground level to give the basement an uninterrupted floor clear of the rail tracks.

Hegeman-Harris had fourteen months to complete the job before handing the finished building over to Frank Lewis by Christmas Day 1936. That would only leave him four weeks to commission all systems before the BIF arrived to start their build-up for a 15 February opening. However, the work seriously overran. The completion deadline was extended on firm undertakings as to time and cost from Hegeman-Harris, neither of which were met according to Earls Court Ltd. Glyn cancelled their contract and appointed others to finish the work. The eventual overshoot of seven months to 'practical completion' in July 1937 arose in part from delayed steel deliveries, as national re-armament had priority. There were many labour difficulties, with twenty-nine unofficial strikes in the first eleven months. Some 800 men – over a quarter of the workforce – downed tools for a fortnight early in the new year.

The all-important LCC licence approval to operate Earls Court was delayed in turn until 6 August. Having cut its moorings at Olympia, the BIF was caught seriously short when it became clear that they would not get in. The British Overseas Trade Board had only weeks to reconfigure and reallocate the entire show after transferring it to White City.

Olympia's Ideal Home had a luckier escape. The show had announced back in October 1936 that it was moving to Earls Court for an April opening in 1937 to coincide with the planned coronation of Edward VIII. Its dates had been specially extended by ten days to take advantage of the enormous crowds expected in London. The show would lavishly reflect a coronation theme (the 'Golden Hall of Homage'), and it also had its 21st anniversary to celebrate. Bulls-eyes all round! Except that the king abdicated on 12 December at about the same time as it became clear that Earls Court would not be ready. Olympia was only too happy to oblige and back there the show went, on earlier dates to catch Easter holidays. The organisers had barely ten weeks to prepare new floorplans and reallocate space, replace the Golden Hall of Homage and rewrite the publicity. The show finally got to Earls Court in 1939.

Earls Court's first event was a Chocolate and Confectionery Exhibition which opened on 1 September. The Motor Show and Commercial Vehicle Show followed despite piles of building material and rubble surrounding the hall and scaffolding covering the entire windowless Warwick Road frontage. Ladies accompanying gentlemen to the Motor Show were admitted free. Sir Malcolm Campbell's record-breaking speedboat *Bluebird* was on show, but Ford of Dagenham's range was exhibited in the specially hired Albert Hall. The Austin Baby 7 was offered for £112; its claimed motoring costs were a penny a mile with four aboard.

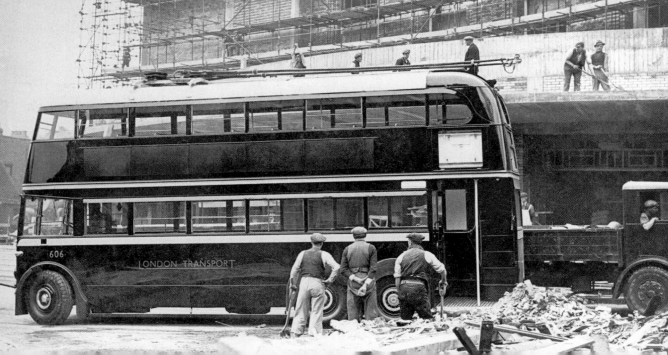

Earls Court's construction was an astonishing achievement but it came at a price – six workmen died during the period. The president of the Society of Engineers is recorded as saying in December 1938 that 'one always found this sort of thing on a work of this kind and, generally speaking, it was taken as a fact that the expenditure of a certain sum of money involved the life of one workman'. He attributed the fatalities to the men's own carelessness. We must not forget them.

The £1.5 million building is still a marvel of technical innovation and flexibility of purpose. Even its thermal heating system was the world's largest. Until 1965 it had its own rail siding for delivery and removal of exhibits and livestock via two lorry lifts to the exhibition floors above.

Any exhibition centre alternates continuously between a building site and a high-class showroom. Earls Court goes one step further. Crane's genius devised a unique 'liquid asset', the 1,800 sq. metre pool in the centre of the main floor. Its 60m × 30m basin is up to 4m deep, and amazingly the 750-ton concrete exhibition floor which covers it when not in use can be removed and reinstated at the push of a button. Crane simply decided to sink the floor to the bottom of the pool. Its three sections can be raised independently to any height up to 5ft above hall floor level in twenty minutes. The hydraulic ram lifting gear still attracts notice from engineers. Four days are needed to pump in 2¼ million gallons, and four more to drain it. Permission must be obtained from the water authority before draining to ensure the weather outlook and sewer capacity are compatible. Even now there is nothing comparable in size or sophistication anywhere.

Frozen assets

In 1927 Claude Langdon, a young impresario in the making, had startled London by introducing motorcycle speedway at the Stamford Bridge football ground not far from Earls Court. His great ambition was to obtain premises for ice-skating and to produce a mammoth ice show. By the early 1930s he acquired what he would later call the Hammersmith Palais. He converted it to an ice-rink and soon became a leading light in British ice hockey circles.

Meanwhile, Lord Lonsdale's National Sporting Club, near-defunct since the First World War, was revived and a new Queensberry boxing tradition became established at the Empress Hall which enjoyed a strong revival in the 1930s. The Club met there for fights every Monday night until the Second World War. Langdon became interested in taking over the hall for ice shows. As Earls Court Ltd had just acquired the lease he met Frank Lewis at the Savoy to cut a deal. Lewis happened to be on the committee of the National Sporting Club and wanted to preserve its Monday meetings while

finding a tenant capable of producing good shows and revenues for the rest of each week. They sat down at 3pm. At 2am next morning Claude Langdon had his hall. It was refurbished and reopened on 1 November with a 1,800 sq. metre ice-rink – bigger than the top Canadian rinks. With seating for 8,000, it was renamed the Empress Stadium ('Hall' to the landlords). Langdon, operating as British Sports Arenas Ltd, built a highly successful operation with ice shows and Christmas ice pantomimes, all-star boxing tournaments, balls, band competitions, badminton championships, reunions and the like.

Lewis wanted a show for the 1938 winter season which would put Earls Court on the map and stretch its capabilities to the limit. It had to be a blockbuster. Langdon had the answer: a gigantic ski-run reaching 100ft into the roof and running out the length of the arena. Lewis formed a company, Earls Court Productions Ltd, to handle this and future light entertainment on the site. Langdon duly submitted his scenario which incorporated a rink beside the run for a complete ice-play titled *Avalanche*. One can only imagine what that entailed, but Lewis's production people turned it down because the cast would have to wear too much clothing. They wanted sex-appeal for the first

Ice King Claude Langdon and 'Belita', c. 1947. Langdon took a lease of the Empress Hall from Earls Court Ltd and staged many successful ice and other shows there until its closure in 1958. *(AC)*

half, without skis. Langdon settled for a 'Winter Cavalcade' to include the summer months. One hundred girls under Miss Bluebell of the Folies Bergère, trapeze artists and performing animals were among the many acts in a worldwide extravaganza.

The second half brought demonstrations on the ski-run including downhill techniques, cross-country meets, snow-shoe races, triple ski-jumping and a history of skiing. Lighting effects included an alpine sunset set to music from *Peer Gynt*. A yodeller was one of many touches of local colour – very local. He was actually a scaffolder from Penge whose repertoire was overheard by Langdon when the slope was under construction. Langdon signed him up on the spot.

The ski-run comprised felted boarding covered in hundreds of tons of crushed ice. One of London's many Italian suppliers of ice blocks was contracted to install it. Two nights before opening Langdon saw to his horror that no ice had yet been laid and a hundred-odd workmen were loafing around a single chugging crusher. He sent stewards round the hall to lock all the doors, told the foreman to complete the

Preparations for Langdon's 'Winter Cavalcade', Earls Court, December 1938. His ski extravaganza required a giant snow slope, here under construction. *(ECO)*

Definitely in the Kiralfy tradition. The completed slope. Boarding on the scaffold framework was covered with felt and hundreds of tons of crushed ice were then laid on. Tree-clad lesser slopes stood to either side. Around 350,000 attended 'Winter Cavalcade'. *(ECO)*

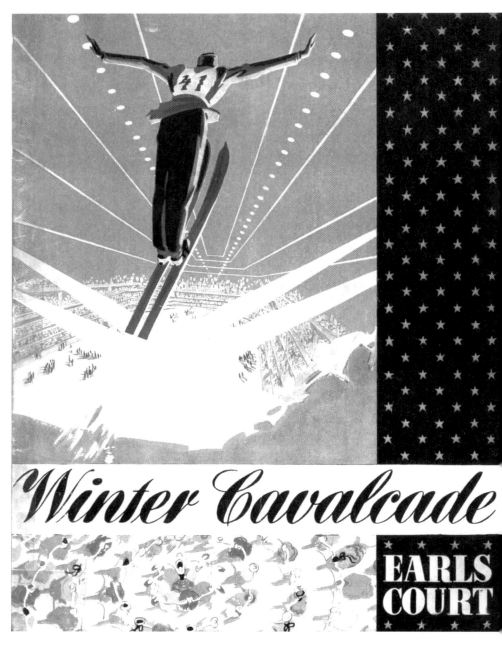

job by morning for rehearsals, and kept them going with trollies of coffee and food. The ice was duly laid and a bonus paid. In spite of the looming war, 350,000 came to see the show.

Boom to bust

A worthy Phoenix had risen from the ashes of the Golden Age. Earls Court Ltd had been incorporated and also officially took over the building from the contractors in July 1937. Exactly two years later the company went into receivership.

EIGHT

HARD TIMES

'I have been trying to promote better trade between [our] two countries in my own little way as an exporter and importer.'

Herr Von Ribbentrop, German Ambassador, addressing British government
and British Industry Fair representatives at Olympia,
22 February 1937

'If there was one night which none of us will ever forget, it was that on which Winston and Mrs Churchill came to Olympia [in 1947]. They arrived when the performance had been in progress about fifteen minutes and as they went to the box the whole audience rose and cheered. The band and even the artistes in the ring had to stop . . . he stopped the show.'

Cyril Mills of Bertram Mills' Circus, memoir

EARLS COURT WAS ON ITS KNEES in 1939, while Olympia reeled from the loss of events to its rival. Philip Hill knew he was going to lose shows to the 'Court' and had formed Exhibitions Ltd in 1936 as an event-organising arm to create replacements. It tried to buy the valuable Building Show from Greville Montgomery in a pre-emptive move, and attempted to stage a film fair. Both endeavours failed, though Montgomery stayed put anyway. Re-formed as Exhibition Promoters (Olympia) Ltd it put on a Woman's Fair with Odhams Press in 1938. This appears to have been its only event, losing the company £33,000.

Cancellation notices for shows at Earls Court and Olympia were readied as Britain prepared for war in July 1939. Sir Oswald Mosley packed Earls Court on the 16th with a final rant appealing to 'this heritage of England . . . struggle . . . sacrifice . . . give to our children . . . sacred gift . . . frail craft across storm-tossed seas . . . the greatest Empire that man has ever seen . . . mighty spirits march beside us . . . be worthy of their company'. The Salvation Army cancelled 25,000 tickets already issued for a celebration at Earls Court to mark General Evangeline Booth's retirement as leader. It was to have been held on Saturday 2 September. Only the day before, a ring of nine designated exit routes out of London came into operation as one-way roads under police control, and the mass evacuation of children began by rail. Radiolympia was open that week, and ended prematurely. Prime Minister Neville Chamberlain declared war on Sunday 3 September.

The British Union of
Fascists' 'Britain First'
meeting, Earls Court,
16 July 1939. Seven
weeks later the country
was at war. (ECO)

The lofty Earls Court was soon requisitioned for the manufacture and repair of London's air defence balloon barrage. Giant 'Blimps' were inflated for testing beneath its 118ft ceiling. The twenty-fifth anniversary of the Soviet Union was celebrated in the Empress Hall in November 1942, attended by the Russian Ambassador and Mme Maisky, Lt Lyudmila Pavlichenko the ace Red Army sniper, and other heroes. A parade of Allied troops and civilian services was followed by patriotic songs to repeated loud applause.

The Empress was later taken over by the Ministry of Aircraft Production for top-secret experimental work. A wind tunnel was built there as a reserve if the pair at Farnborough were bombed. It tested some of Sir Frank Whittle's first jet engines, its own howling turbine bedded in concrete on Claude Langdon's wrecked rink. Winston Churchill was there to see the first demonstration of FIDO, the flarepath blind-landing-in-fog device which was too secret to test in the blackout on an airfield. Some of the seating was ripped out to simulate a 400ft runway beside which FIDO's pipes were laid. On ignition the fog-dispersing flames rose gratifyingly roofwards.

Neither building suffered damage during the war but West Brompton station opposite was destroyed by incendiary bombs.

All change

Olympia was requisitioned by the War Office on 10 January 1940 as civilian internment camp No. 14, paying an annual rent of £32,500. During the Dunkirk evacuation in May/June that year the hall was General Charles de Gaulle's assembly point for what became the Free French Army. The Royal Army Service Corps then took it over as a transport depot until October 1944 when Olympia became a clothing store, and finally a demobilisation centre, in which role it served until 23 March 1946. Olympia was itself demobbed on 30 June. The place was in very poor shape and had suffered light bomb damage on six occasions. Addison Road station alongside was badly knocked about in raids on 19/20/21 October 1940, closing the line. A V1 flying bomb fell in Russell Road on the other side of the station on 30 June 1944, injuring eight people, severely damaging the platform canopies and holing Olympia's roof. The station was renamed Kensington (Olympia) after rebuilding in 1946.

Olympia's chairmanship had passed to board member Louis Nicholas after Philip Hill's death in 1944. Reginald Heaton retired in 1947 in poor health after thirty-five years as managing director. He had created the wonderful International Horse Shows of the early years and had battled beside Hill in holding the fort against Earls Court. Sadly, he died the following year. 'Cockie' Cochran had received a knighthood. He died most tragically in 1951 aged seventy-nine. He was taking a bath when he suffered an arthritic spasm and was unable to reach to turn off a scalding tap. His cries were not heard in time. Each man in his own way had contributed greatly to Olympia's past success.

Times were changing. The pre-war protectionist nature of many European trade exhibitions, which favoured their domestic industries over foreign participation, was evolving into a more open global approach to commerce. The mammoth all-industries national trade fairs across Europe were in decline, replaced by smaller specialist shows serving specific industries and open to the healthy stimulus of foreign participation. The insular BIF trundled on, filling Earls Court and Olympia from 1947 until 1956, but sections were already splitting away to form their own trade shows. Over the next thirty-five years literally hundreds of exhibitions emerged and flourished in Britain under independent or trade association control. They generated high demand for the country's limited purpose-built space. Until Birmingham's National Exhibition Centre opened in 1976, London's two big halls enjoyed a captive market.

Captive it may have been, but Earls Court became trapped in a downward spiral. Its badly knocked about halls needed heavy and sustained investment for repairs and improvements. It was being run by receivers paid only to keep the front door open and the lights working until the place could be sold. A 'Catch 22' situation developed. Event organisers refused to pay a premium on rental until the premises improved, and significant improvement was impossible without the premium income. Worse, as the exhibition hall's amenities and condition fell further behind its competitors at home and abroad, some major organisers demanded reduced rentals which worsened the situation. Britain's biggest shop window, Earls Court, and to a lesser extent Olympia, fell increasingly behind its continental rivals in equipment, hall services and quality of management, although paradoxically both were among the most intensively used centres in Europe.

Successive governments remained indifferent, refusing to recognise that modern well-equipped exhibition centres are vital to the national economy and are hugely expensive to build and maintain in what is only a seasonal business. They preferred to encourage and generously fund British firms to exhibit at overseas fairs, principally in Germany, where national and regional governments knew the value of a strong exhibitions base in generating overseas sales and invisible earnings, and invested directly in it.

It is against this background that we follow the postwar fortunes of the two London centres.

Circus

Bertram Mills' Circus returned for Christmas 1946 as Olympia's first postwar event. A weary public hungry for entertainment flooded the box office with postal bookings. Cyril Mills opened it up a fortnight early in anticipation, but instead of a few extra bags of mail he received three van-loads on the first day! The avalanche continued, and when the office first opened to callers on 2 December the queue stretched far down Kensington High Street. It was still 150yd long at 8pm. Every performance sold out before opening night. Audiences cheered themselves hoarse for the six-week run.

An accident at Bertram Mills' Circus Funfair, Olympia, 1956/7 season. The Ferris wheel's axle snapped with passengers aboard. All got down safely. *(ECO)*

Bertram Mills came back each year until television and other distractions finally brought the circus's last season at Olympia in 1965/6. It was also to be the last appearance for Cyril and Bernard Mills. The brothers had little option but to sell the business while it was still a going concern. The high point that winter was undoubtedly a children's charity concert attended by the Queen and Prince Philip, the Prince of Wales and Princess Anne, Princess Margaret and other members of the royal family. The finale came with the last act – a flying trapeze with the Gaonas. It was planned that Victor Gaona should attempt a triple somersault into the hands of his father. The feat had not been achieved at Olympia since 1925. Victor had consistently done it in rehearsal, but he only had two chances. He could afford a net-fall the first time, but a second fall would kill his professional reputation. The moment came – he fell. At the second attempt the high trapeze took its two great swings as 7,000 spectators willed him to succeed. He spun and was caught – and the audience went wild. Not even the Mills brothers knew that Victor had deliberately thrown that first somersault to heighten the tension. It demonstrated his supreme self-confidence that he should rest his future on the final make-or-break attempt. It was a fitting end to the last of Olympia's wonderful shows with the Mills family.

Although the circus returned in 1967 it was under new ownership and the Mills family was not a part of it. It could never be the same, and did not come again.

'Ideal Home' moves house

Back to 1947, when the Ideal Home Exhibition and the still mighty BIF followed the circus into Olympia. The *Daily Mail* show was confronted by austerity, rationing and shortages, not least in the national housing stock. Food, clothing and petrol remained on coupons. Restaurant meals were price-capped at five shillings. Meat, bacon, butter, cheese, tea, sugar and sweets only came off the ration in 1952. Supplies of house coal and tobacco were hard to find. Furniture and much else for home consumption was only available in 'Utility' form. Cars, Scotch whisky, all luxury goods and fashions were 'export only'. The suitably austere chancellor, Stafford Cripps, was 'a strange monastic-

'The Unplanned Garden', Building Exhibition, Olympia, 1947. An ironic exhibit such as this sticks in the mind long after conventional displays are forgotten. *(Montgomery Exhibitions)*

A packed Ideal Home show in 1959. Olympia was transformed into a Cotswold village of full-scale houses and shops, backed by a stylised Blenheim Palace. *(ECO)*

looking man' according to Harold Macmillan, 'emaciated and said to live off watercress grown off the blotting paper on his desk'. The nation longed for better times.

Ideal Home tried hard to show the way. Acute shortages of traditional building materials led to the ingenious use of alternatives for mass-produced factory-prefabricated homes. Six versions of these boxy and very basic 'prefabs' comprised 'The Village of Beginning Again', one of them an all-aluminium shell made by the aircraft industry for the Ministry of Supply. They were far superior to slum properties and bomb-damaged housing and remained surprisingly popular for years. A new section was devoted to children rather than just babies because a generation of youngsters had missed out on so much in the war. A wonderfully escapist feature was the display of replica film sets from past favourites. It was repeated the next year with examples from ballerina Moira Shearer's *The Red Shoes*, David Lean's *Oliver Twist*, *Miranda* and Laurence Olivier's *Hamlet*.

By the 'Swinging Sixties' all was transformed. The young had money to spend. Household and leisure choices had never been so wide or so achievable. 'The Islands of Leisure' feature in the Grand Hall in 1965 comprised a 55ft-diameter lake with nine floating islands each themed to a different recreation. They could be called up to come alongside for closer inspection by pressing a numbered button, and included Lazing in the Sun, Dinner for Two, Pop Session, Evening at Home – with TV, and Time to Relax –

in the Bathroom. Attendances in those days were so great that in the crush it could become impossible even to raise an arm in the main aisles. To get inside the show houses meant a wait of one or two hours. The imaginatively landscaped centrepieces and the show's presentation set standards which remain unsurpassed.

Ideal Home crossed to Earls Court in 1979 for more space. The advantages of the great pool were not overlooked. The biggest bathroom in the world was the central feature in 1996. A vast bath with 12ft-high chrome taps actually dwarfed the two canal barges floating in it. An en suite washbasin over 30ft high stood against a tiled wall to scale, with racked toothbrushes like bristled bargepoles. It is this sense of fun alongside the practical that keeps the show fresh and makes it the national institution it is.

'Just add water'. The Ideal Home show's move to Earls Court meant it could utilise the 2¼ million gallon pool, used here in 1985. *(ECO)*

Earls Court captures 'The Smithfield'

Earls Court was de-requisitioned late in 1946. It was the subject of a dispute between the British Overseas Airways Corporation and the Board of Trade. BOAC wanted the building to become 'the biggest and finest air traffic centre in the world'. It would be the new Heathrow airport's passenger and freight terminal with ample check-in facilities and customer services, offices for all airlines using the airport, and a direct rail link to Heathrow. The BoT disagreed, wanting the building for its original purpose.

Despite the uncertainties of receivership Earls Court won important new shows following a thin start in 1947 when only the BIF, an assembly of Jehovah's Witnesses and the Motor Show appeared. An Aquashow the following year starred Johnny 'Tarzan' Weissmuller and Esther Williams in one of the pool's surprisingly few such productions. The Royal Smithfield Show came across from Islington's Aggie in 1949, and the Royal Tournament and Radiolympia (renamed the Radio Show) followed in 1950. The first two were desperate for space, while the Radio Show needed a date change which Olympia could not accommodate. The receivers cracked their knuckles anxiously as they still awaited a buyer for the business.

Meat and veg do not mix at Earls Court's Smithfield Show. A Vegetarian Society demo outside the gates, 1979. *(The Times)*

The Smithfield Show was born in December 1799. It was held at Wooton's Livery Stables near London's Smithfield Meat Market 'to ascertain what form of livestock husbandry gives most meat to man'. Prize money totalled £52. Pigs were added in 1800 and carcasses followed in 1895. Arguments between breeders and butchers as to what should constitute a champion ran on well into the nineteenth century.

After several moves the growing show took itself to the Aggie in 1862, offering over £2,000 in prize money. Its move to Earls Court in 1949 was accompanied by members of the Agricultural Engineers' Association and the Society of Motor Manufacturers and Traders. The alliance made sense. A postwar increase in farming mechanisation and the worldwide shortage of equipment had brought implements and machinery to the fore. Britain ranked second only to the USA in farm equipment manufacture. The first items to be exhibited at Smithfield, in 1806, had been a range of chaff cutters. They were followed by machines making land-drains, hay tedders, sail reaping machines, reaper binders, threshing tackle and stationary steam engines, little fixed-drawbar tractors, the

first combines, and eventually by today's huge microchipped air-conditioned 15-acres-a-day wonders with whispering servos and multi-hosed hydraulics, bouncing along on balloon tyres half as high as haystacks, the driver remote and soundproofed in an executive armchair behind tinted glass with Stravinsky on the stereo — maybe!

Farmers and others from the meat and machinery sectors descend with their families on Earls Court's Smithfield Show each year for a glorious few days of earthy gossip, competition and shopping, joined by many townsfolk. The late November timing traditionally signals the end of autumn cultivation and the peak of condition of the fatstock. Young Farmers' Clubs are there in droves and the bars at Earls Court used to dispense more beer at this show than at all the others combined.

The Queen Mother was a devoted follower of the show, attending without fail every year and knowledgeably discussing with breeders and judges the finer points of steers and sheep in the ring. The author saw her in her nineties gaily doing business with leading stockbreeders over lunch and enjoying every minute.

A done deal in 1979 — the Smithfield Show renews its contract for more years at Earls Court. Left to right: A.S.R. Austin (Royal Smithfield Club), James Stobo (Chairman, RSC), Major-General Peter Blunt (MD, Earls Court Olympia), Leonard Potter (Show Chairman), Harold Bennison (Vice-President, Agricultural Engineers' Association), Gerry Kunz (Show Organiser). *(ECO)*

The Queen Mother never failed to visit the Smithfield Show, here inspecting the Supreme Champion in 1982. *(Press Association)*

The Empress

The Empress Hall had a final postwar flowering with Claude Langdon's many promotions and popular Christmas shows. As Britain's King of the Ice Shows for over twenty years he matched Kiralfy in filling the place to the walls with deceptive ease. He had introduced the idea of Christmas pantomime on ice before the war, with speech and song and a storyline. Langdon's 'Cinderella on Ice' was the first rink show to synchronise sound with light effects. Talking of which, a *Times* reviewer of another Langdon production noted sardonically that 'the masterpiece of *décor* is the gigantic shadow of the electrician at his dimmers which appears over the proscenium arch with all the unrehearsed beauty of an effect in a Russian theatre'.

When the Royal Philharmonic Orchestra came to the Empress Hall in February 1949 under Sir Thomas Beecham, the maestro walked out on Langdon at rehearsal and refused to perform, saying he had been deceived. All 130 musicians followed him. A hockey match so closely preceded the concert that time did not allow construction of a platform and conductor's rostrum above the rink until just before the actual performance. Rehearsal had to take place on boards laid directly on the ice. Beecham believed this was all he was getting. He returned the next day after the

The Lillie Road entrance to Empress Hall, c. 1935. (H&FA)

The site of the old Earls Court exhibition grounds in 1948. Only the Empress Hall remains *(bottom left)*. The Western Gardens are built over, and a war-battered Earls Court 1 fills the triangle *(right)*. *(Simmons Aerofilms)*

Rock'n'Roll fans at Empress Hall, October 1956. American band leader Lionel Hampton tries to leave the stage. The Albert Hall cancelled his booking there the following week after learning that he would include rock numbers. (*The Times*)

misunderstanding was corrected, while Langdon's staff frantically recalled the scattered musicians by telegram. The large audience heard what *The Times* next day considered to be 'an impassioned performance . . . and what may well have been the most exciting "1812" ever heard'.

'Babes in the Wood' in 1950 typified Claude's approach to spectacle. Skating naturally, but with a flying ballet; an ensemble in the dark with luminescent cloaks for the dancers; real horses – on ice! – and a motor bike, a car *and* an aircraft. An archery contest for the Nottingham Fair scene? Get me real archers. Music? The Dagenham Girl Pipers, of course.

The immortal Sonja Henie had revolutionised ice-skating both technically and with her daring costumes, only modestly revealing by today's standards. She skated often for Langdon and last appeared at the Empress Hall in 1953 for the Ice Revue, one of London's outstanding spectacles that Coronation year. Other post-war presentations ranged through all-star boxing, concerts by the London Symphony Orchestra with renowned soloists such as Kirsten Flagstad, the *Daily Herald* national band award, The

Olympia in the 1950s. The ugly covered way, since removed, masks much of the attractive façade. *(ECO)*

Star balls and *Melody Maker*'s National Award Concerts, the All-England Badminton Championships (and, needless to say, badminton on ice), 'Hiawatha', the Alamein Reunion attended by Winston Churchill and Field-Marshal Montgomery, and the Conservative Party rally where Churchill as Leader of the Opposition made rousing speeches.

A rock 'n' roll concert by the American Lionel Hampton and his band in 1956 certainly rocked London. A twenty-year actors' union ban on American musicians had just been lifted and public eagerness to see the group 'live' was intense. The tour had already brought baton-wielding police on to the streets of Paris to control wild crowds, and tear gas had to be used in Stockholm. Hampton's frenzied style has been likened to a runaway train. When he unwisely led his group into the audience at the Empress they were mobbed, the commissionaires struggling to get them back on to the stage. As Hampton said later: 'They were only having fun and this is the 1956 way of doing it.' It was not the Albert Hall's way – that same day Hampton's forthcoming concert there was cancelled. He died aged ninety-four in 2002.

Huge crowds – looming clouds

Olympia reported 1953/4 to be its best financial year since the war, with pre-tax profits of £220,000. A stand-fitting and electrical contracting department was contributing usefully. But industrial unrest and union militancy were a national problem. Exhibitions were a natural target as they are time-critical and easily picketed. The annual marketing effort of an entire industry could be put at risk or wrecked, losing precious orders and damaging employment prospects across the country. When 3,000 painters, electricians and carpenters struck simultaneously in 1949 during the construction of Radiolympia and Earls Court's Motor Show, exhibitor-managers and their staffs in both halls struggled to complete the work themselves. The Radio Show

announced that it would open even if exhibits had to be laid out on the floor. The unions called off the strike only a few hours before the joint opening. The Radio Show opened in 1953 in semi-darkness with many exhibits lacking power during a day-long guerrilla action by electricians. A national electricians' strike in February 1954 cancelled Crufts Dog Show and caused the Ideal Home Show and Olympia serious losses. Much worse lay ahead.

The 1953 Motor Show opened early on police instructions when a queue ten deep doubled back down Philbeach Gardens while another obstructed traffic in Brompton Road, their combined length totalling 1 mile. By 11am 130,310 visitors had been admitted and the show cars remained visible only from the gallery. Movement around the hall was almost impossible.

The first Food Fair opened at Olympia in 1950 to run biennially in even years as a hugely popular show until 1968. The Hotel, Restaurant and Catering Exhibition launched in 1948 (later renamed Hotelympia) was another big biennial event, held in even years well into the 1980s. An annual highlight was the *Salon Culinaire*, the focus of competitions to test the highest levels of catering craftsmanship. Spectators sat theatre-style before a row of demonstration kitchens with giant overhead mirrors. Chefs from all over Britain and abroad competed for highly valued awards in many categories in senior and junior Salons. A party from a Kenya college were notable successes in 1978. Happily for Olympia's annual accounts, Montgomery's biennial Building Show fell in the odd years.

Jack Hylton's Earls Court Circus was another crowd-puller, its acts in 1952 including human cannonballs Leo Dinant and 'Miss Atomia'. They were fired together from a single barrel into a net 100ft away, twice daily. The Poli Orea dogs included a black rebel which was shot for disobedience, only to escape from his coffin and slyly join his own funeral procession. Miss Isolina perched on a wire-borne chair under the roof while using both hands to play 'Torrento' on a violin – many in the audience used both hands to cover their eyes. Less successful was trick motorcyclist Jacques Minerva the following year – he was run over by his own machine, 24ft above the ring. He finished the performance before collapsing and being taken to hospital, his helmet 'murderously dented'.

The 1953 Radio Show's BBC television studio at Earls Court demonstrated how productions were

Popular public shows drew immense numbers in the postwar years. This queue at Olympia in 1954 is at least 200yd long, doubling back down Joseph Emberton's ghastly covered way which was tacked on in 1936, seriously damaging much of Olympia's Italianate frontage. The covered way has since been replaced by a landscaped approach. *(ECO)*

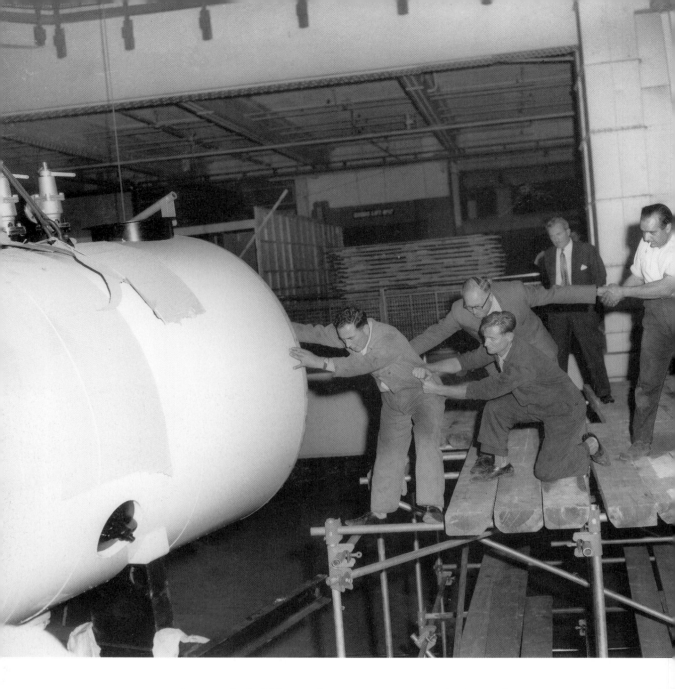

Whoops! These men are above the Empire Hall's open well, two floors up and trying to swing the hoisted boiler exhibit on to (or off if the show is over) a flimsy staging. The balcony rail has been removed. Such risk-taking is unthinkable today. *(ECO)*

staged. A 21ft monitor screen mounted above the set was an eye-opening improvement on the average domestic 14-inch set. Attendance that year exceeded 295,000 over ten days.

The Boat Show

The first National Boat Show was staged at Olympia's four-storey Empire Hall in 1955. It was not the most appropriate accommodation but it made a promising start. More light craft must have gone up the open well on the end of a rope than ever got into the goods lifts. The Hon. Max Aitken, a keen sailor whose father Lord Beaverbrook owned the *Daily Express* newspaper, had persuaded the paper to sponsor the show by guaranteeing the first £2,000 of any losses. There was no risk of that when over 120,000 people attended. The partnership continued until 1988.

There were bizarre difficulties. The Boat Show adjoined Bertram Mills' Circus in the main hall, with a shared covered service road between them. This was part-occupied by lion cages and elephant pens (only the road drains were large enough to cope). The constant roaring and trumpeting hardly chimed with Boat Show visitors' mind-pictures of seagulls and the plash of waves. The smells memorably permeated the whole building. The show moved to Earls Court in 1960 where for the first time large fully rigged craft floated inside the hall, although it was not the first time that boats had been displayed on that spot.

Craft were exhibited for sale on water in *precisely* this location nearly sixty years before. In March 1902 the Thames Boatbuilders' Protection Association hired the Warwick Road end of the present site for a Boating Exhibition in the Ducal and Prince's Halls and on the lake beyond them. Today's pool overlies the old lake. *The Times* reported:

Boat Show magic in wintry London, 1967. (ECO)

More Boat Show magic in wintry London. *(ECO)*

All the principal makers on the Thames seemed to be represented. Skiffs and gigs and punts and dinghies; racing boats, sailing boats, motor boats; steam launches, petrol pinnaces, Canadian canoes; oars, sculls, paddles – every kind of river craft and all sorts of propelling appliances can be seen and compared.

Applications were invited for a return in 1903. The boatbuilders were subsequently divided, the motor boat fraternity becoming junior partners of the SMMT, whose Motor Shows welcomed them on condition they exhibited nowhere else. The SMMT married sky with water in 1914 with its Aero and Marine Exhibition at Olympia. The boatbuilders reunited in 1922 at the first London Boat Show at Islington's Aggie. After three years the Depression and the war killed it. The Empire Hall event followed.

Attendance at the first Earls Court show leapt to 320,000. The exhibitors took home £5m of orders – and an enterprising thief took home a £45,000 boat ready-loaded on a trailer. By the millennium the industry was spending £4m to stage the exhibition, but it generated sixteen times that figure in direct orders. The ocean-going craft for the pool were dispatched from the yards on huge road transporters to a strict arrival schedule with police escort, travelling through London streets cleared of impeding road 'furniture' before marshalling at the hall, and on into the water in strict sequence. If any missed their designated arrival slot, then like the Berlin airlift, they had to return to base.

The Boat Show's traditional lunches gave the industry an opportunity to influence governments and sponsors. Prime Minister Edward Heath caught a blast in the 1970s when he extolled his government's record of support for the marine industry. David Sanders the Boat Show chairman disagreed, observing pointedly that the consumer credit restrictions were doing more harm to the industry than the notorious three-day weeks of 1973 when Heath confronted the unions. As the Prime Minister spluttered in protest his Chancellor, sitting on Sanders' other side, dug him in the ribs and whispered 'Keep going – you're right!' The restrictions were lifted a few months later. The show was the first Earls Court exhibition to open on a Sunday, after the British Marine Industries Federation led a successful campaign to overcome the Sunday Trades Act in the 1980s. So many people turned up that every turnstile and ticket window in the building had to be staffed to prevent overcrowding and closure of Earls Court station.

The high point of the 1985 show was the Royal Navy's dizzying 'Manning the Mast' ceremony. It was performed by 100 ratings whose synchronised climbing of the rigging on an 80ft mainmast was accompanied by the beat of drums. When they were spread across each tier, a 'Button Boy' finally mounted the tip of the mast to stand bravely on a 6-inch plinth and give the Salute.

The Boat Show has been to Earls Court what Bertram Mills' Circus was to Olympia – a winter heart-warmer for millions.

Chips with everything

Olympia hosted the first computer exhibition in Europe in 1958. The historic British Electronic Computer Exhibition and Symposium opened on 28 November in the National Hall with forty-two exhibitors. Everything there represented ten years of achievement from scratch. Before 1948 there was nothing to work from. The top-secret wartime equipment developed at Bletchley Park was still unknown to the commercial world, yet this show was already presenting the third generation of transistorised computer technology. The symposium was even more important than the exhibition in providing a forum for exchange of information. The event was organised by Mrs Sarah Elliott MBE, newly elected chairman of the Association of Exhibition Organisers, and exhibition director of the Office Appliance and Business Equipment Trades Association.

From then on Olympia became a favoured platform for the industry's exhibitions. The world's smallest Bible was shown for the first time at the 1964 Business Efficiency Exhibition. It was a matchbox-sized plastic card from the National Cash Register Company containing micro-images of every page of the Old and New Testaments. Ten years later it was replaced by a micro-dot. COMPEC for computer peripherals and software first opened in 1971 and became Britain's major exhibition in this field. By 1983 it had 500 exhibitors, a 40 per cent growth over the previous year, filling every corner.

Sister Mary's Jaguar. The Sister Superior of an Exeter convent won a 4-litre Jaguar Mk X at the 1966 Hotelympia. She exchanged it for a smaller car and a cheque. (The Times)

Breezy entrepreneur Evan Steadman stepped in to launch a string of computer-related exhibitions in the 1970s, later bringing them to Olympia 2 and opening others there. The author remembers him addressing his exhibitors after one successful show, though not in the customarily deferential terms of 'hope we shall have the pleasure of welcoming you back next time'. Steadman gave it straight: 'I know you've had a b—y good show – so have I. You've paid for my new Roller outside. You can pat it when you leave.' They loved it and happily signed up for space again.

The stand manager of a famous Italian office equipment company came white-faced to tell the author at one of Steadman's shows that their records of buyer and enquirer visitors for the past four days had been stolen. It transpired that the documents were kept in a wastepaper basket on the stand – a cleaner had noticed the full basket, and emptied it. The shattered stand staff spent a fruitless morning scaling Olympia's waste mountain.

The rivals

Earls Court changed hands in November 1955 when a re-formed Earls Court Ltd led by chairman Harold Drayton acquired the assets. General manager Stanley Baker was replaced by the charismatic Major-General W.H.D. 'Dick' Ritchie in 1957. Frank Lewis, acclaimed 'a tower of strength in the exhibition and show world' by Claude Langdon, stayed on and joined the board. (He became chairman in 1965.) They had much to do. Bookings at Empress Hall were down to little more than a darts competition and a few 'one-day stands' after Langdon's next Christmas ice show. The grand old lady finally expired in the summer of 1958 and the contents were auctioned off. It was a sad but inevitable end for the last functioning link with the Golden Age.

Ritchie produced a development scheme to replace the Empress with a huge new hall, doubling Earls Court's letting space to 93,000 sq. metres. It would extend beyond the central 'island' into the coal yards and included parking for 6,000 cars. His plan was received coolly by the Board of Trade in 1959. The LCC was more concerned to build a hall at the Crystal Palace, though nothing came of it.

Earls Court Ltd and newly formed Atrium Properties secured planning consent to erect the 300ft Empress State Building on the site of the old hall. Designed by Stone Toms & Partners, it would be one of the tallest office blocks in London at that time and was completed in 1962. Earls Court retained its leasehold interest in the 6-acre site until 1969 when Land Securities Investment Trust bought it.

There was much speculation in 1969 that a National Exhibition Centre would be built at London's old Northolt airport, but the rival scheme near Birmingham was favoured by the Labour government and won the day. For some time Olympia Ltd had been actively diversifying out of exhibitions as a hedge against future trouble from any quarter. It foresaw a price war between the London and Birmingham centres, and prepared to redevelop Olympia in that eventuality before making for the exit. But first it sounded out Earls Court about an alliance between the two – in effect a reverse take-over of Earls Court. The 'village hall' waited two years for a response. It came in

the spring of 1971. Earls Court's still financially strapped company, newly chaired by Ritchie on Frank Lewis's retirement, would go it alone.

Bigger fish circled Olympia Ltd. Property developer Sir Robin McAlpine increased his stake to 18 per cent of the company in 1971. Thoroughly alarmed that redevelopment would blow out the Ideal Home Exhibition, the Daily Mail Group increased its holding to 28 per cent in a race to control Olympia.

The Birmingham initiative was equally bad news for the powerful Association of Exhibition Organisers. The AEO had been calling for a London-based NEC. They urged that Earls Court and Olympia should merge under a single management and build smaller linking halls on the railway land between them. They certainly got the merger. It came within two years, but for quite different reasons. A seemingly less-than-white knight rode in from nowhere, spearing both halls on the end of his lance.

NINE

STERLING ACHIEVEMENT

'In its way, the Earls Court Olympia complex of exhibition halls is a great commercial feat. In most of the rest of Europe it is the pattern for governments or regional authorities to pour public money into developing exhibition facilities. They realise that exhibitions attract visitors, who then spend money. . . . Even in the United States most exhibition halls are municipally supported. Not so with Earls Court Olympia . . . which has to pay its way.'

Derek Harris, The Times, 16 October 1991

THE NEAR-SIMULTANEOUS confirmation early in 1972 that the National Exhibition Centre was to be built near Birmingham and that a developer had swallowed Earls Court left the exhibition industry in a state of confusion.

The first news of the takeover had come in City reports at the end of January that property tycoon Jeffrey Sterling's Sterling Guarantee Trust (SGT) had made a bid of £4.4m for the 'Court'. His objectives became clearer a week later when he also bought McAlpine's stake in Olympia. The Earls Court bid was accepted on 23 March. SGT speedily announced plans for redevelopment of the 17.7-acre site in alliance with Town and City Properties (T&C). They were already in talks with London Transport about varying the Earls Court lease which had seventy years to run, and were inviting it to include its adjoining 15 acres in a single massive £50m development.

Having bought Earls Court, SGT planned to sell off the venue's property assets to a new development company jointly owned with T&C for a reported £7.5m cash. The deal represented a healthy profit and they would still have a 40 per cent stake in the subsequent development. The implications left most London exhibition organisers anxiously preparing Plan B. A mass exodus of London's trade fairs to Birmingham became a racing certainty pending clarification from Sterling.

In the general upheaval J. Lyons announced it would redevelop its 10-acre Blythe Road site opposite Olympia. The Cadby Hall HQ and food factory were to move elsewhere. This was Olympia's last chance to expand hugely but expensively, bridging Blythe Road at gallery level to double its letting space. The NEC had got in first, and expansion was the last thought on the company's mind.

SGT successfully bid £11.4m for Olympia in March 1973 after buying the Daily Mail Group's holding. In return SGT had guaranteed it continuity and space for the Ideal

Home Show until 1988. Sterling revealed that the Olympia site would be redeveloped for other purposes after the Earls Court building had been converted to mixed use with a much smaller but modern exhibition hall. Large events such as the Motor Show and the Tournament were expected to move to Birmingham, while others could occupy Olympia pending completion of the new Earls Court. Olympia would then close for good.

This carefully laid strategy was ready to roll when the oil crisis broke. The producing countries collaborated to turn their natural resources into an economic weapon, controlling oil and gas supplies to the west and greatly increasing prices. The crisis built over the summer and merged with trade union objections to a government-imposed prices and incomes policy. It came to a head in November with a miners' overtime ban just as winter set in, government cuts in fuel oil and petrol deliveries, and a 50mph limit on all roads. Petrol rationing coupons were issued but never used. The economy crashed and property values went down with it. Jeffrey Sterling's scheme was expensively stalled.

Diversions

A big Soviet Exhibition at Earls Court in August 1968 had been brought to its knees when Russia invaded Czechoslovakia part-

way through the event. Some 2,000 student demonstrators picketed the Warwick Road entrance with placards stating 'Trade Enquiries for Tanks – All Fully Tested on Allies', and 'Monster Exhibition'. The gates were closed after a Russian flag was burned, and inside the hall a full-size Russian show house was set on fire overnight. The exhibition followed a similar show there in 1961, and a third came to the Court in 1979. It was remembered largely for Dima, the 40,000-year-old baby mammoth discovered in permafrost. At the main entrance observant visitors noticed that a giant photograph of former Foreign Secretary David Owen shaking hands with Prime Minister Kosygin simultaneously showed Kosygin standing behind Owen smiling knowingly.

One of Earls Court's more unusual spectacles involved the counting of Greater London's votes in the 1975 referendum on joining the EEC. Some 750 trestle tables in four lines were manned by an army of counters on one side and almost as many observers on the other, including Jackie Dash, the firebrand leader of the London dockers who was firmly anti-EEC. At 7pm the result of the Earls Court count was announced:

YES: 2,201,031
NO: 1,100,185

Crowds filing into the 1976 Motor Show stared at a wheel-less red £6,000 Lotus Elite 501 on blocks in the forecourt. A poster listed over a hundred complaints from its owner David Ayers of Twickenham. His plan worked. Embarrassed Lotus officials hurried out with offers of a complete overhaul and a loan car. A 25-year-old model was less successful in 1971 when claiming for an injury to her left breast incurred as she clambered from a car roof – a silicone implant allegedly shifted. The judge decided she was the architect of her own misfortune as 'with all those men standing round her I find it inconceivable that she did not seek their help'.

Merger and new management

Jeffrey (now Lord) Sterling kept the two halls open through the Black Winter of 1973/4, its many three-day weeks of power rationing, and the mineworkers' actions that felled Edward Heath's government in March 1974. Sterling could have ridden out the crashed property market by closing the heavily loss-making Earls Court, but it was a live national asset and such action was unthinkable. A property upturn was probably several years distant. Sterling could only move forward by making a go of the halls as show centres. He merged them into Earls Court and Olympia Ltd (ECO), removed the rigidities that accumulate over time in a sellers' market, and began to rebuild the business. He secured Town and City Properties after a reverse takeover of SGT. Sterling now had a clear road ahead and a radically new destination.

Nice bike. Photocall at the Motorcycle Show, Earls Court, 1979. *(ECO)*

Queues entering the first Motorfair, an in-house ECO event, at Earls Court in 1977 after the SMMT Motor Show moved to Birmingham. *(ECO)*

Festival of Mind, Body and Spirit, Olympia, 1984. Launched in 1976, the show quickly built a devoted following for the more way-out religious, health and free-thinking groups. *(ECO)*

ECO chairman Christopher Stewart-Smith must be credited with the introduction of the strategy which eventually broke the impasse between static or even falling rentals and the pressing need to fund expensive hall improvements. He got rid of Olympia's hedge investments in a timber company and property, gave Leslie Overs' successful Electrical Services contracting division its head (Overs joined the board of ECO), put a strong manager into the stand-fitting company and extended event contracting services into new fields. Like Hill before him he had to make new shows in anticipation of losses when Birmingham's NEC opened its doors. Philbeach Events Ltd was later formed for this purpose, led successfully by the intrepid David 'give it a punt' Fasken, who later became ECO Group's managing director and deputy chairman.

But first, a critical loss of confidence had to be overcome. The exhibition industry was wary of promises from a property developer turned saviour, and Sterling could only put up £1.5m to start an Earls Court improvement programme. It was not enough to demonstrate long-term commitment once the property market recovered. For that reason alone, at least one big international trade fair hesitated to book into the hall, while others were already leaving ECO for Birmingham. The turning point came in July 1979 when the Greater London Council contributed £5m, to be repaid when later profits reached an agreed level. The gesture was hugely significant. It was a tangible expression of confidence from outside the T&C camp that the halls had a durable future. The GLC money and Stewart-Smith's initiatives primed a halls 'Facelift' programme which eventually unlocked frozen rental tariffs to fund some £80m of major improvements.

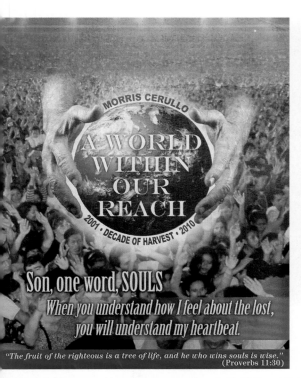

Son, one word, SOULS
When you understand how I feel about the lost, you will understand my heartbeat.

"The fruit of the righteous is a tree of life, and he who wins souls is wise."
(Proverbs 11:30)

Left: The Morris Cerullo show, Earls Court, 2002. *(ECO)*
Above: Masons Grand Lodge, Earls Court, 1992. *(ECO)*
Below: Billy Graham at Earls Court, 1966. 27,000 attended on a single night. *(ECO)*

Building the four-level stage with its moving stairways for Harvey Goldsmith's *Aida* at Earls Court, 1988. Audiences averaged nearly 15,000 for each of the seven performances by a cast of over 600. *Carmen* followed in 1989 and *Tosca* two years later. *(ECO)*

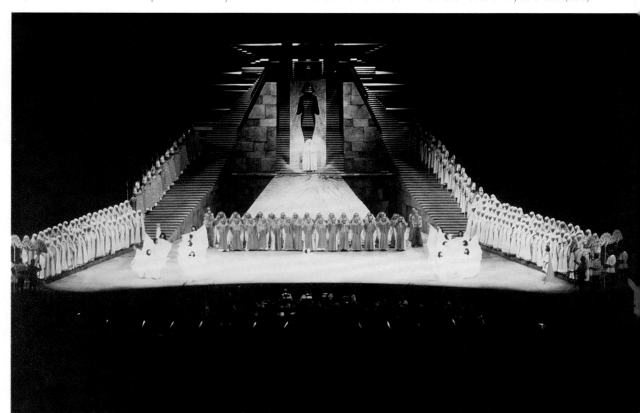

One of the most striking treatments of Earls Court's entrance, the carousel for the first Motorfair, 1977. *(ECO)*

Part of a fine centrepiece at the Daily Mail Ideal Home Exhibition, Earls Court, 1982. *(ECO)*

International Menswear Fair, Earls Court, 1987. *(ECO)*

International Jewellery London, Earls Court 2, 2001. *(ECO)*

A stand at International Menswear, Earls Court, 1979. *(ECO)*

The British Designer Show at Olympia, 1984. Walking the walk in the Pillar Hall, and resting the feet in Olympia 2. *(ECO)*

The £100m Earls Court 2 hall going up in August 1990. The West London line and space for a motorway run beneath. The Empress State Building on the left overlies the old Empress Hall. The first event at EC2 was the London Boat Show in January 1991. *(ECO)*

London Boat Show,
Earls Court.
*(centre, ECO; top and
bottom, National Boat
Shows Ltd)*

The team – Earls Court and Olympia Group, 2002. *(ECO)*

The importance of this windfall was lost on at least one individual who should have known better. When the GLC deputy leader and Stewart-Smith announced the new funding at a presentation on 'Facelift' to leaders of the exhibition industry, SMMT Motor Show organiser Gerry Kunz was the first to raise his hand. To general astonishment he launched into a trivial tirade concerning the removal of a small bar somewhere in the vastness of Earls Court!

Before the gain came the pain. The NEC had opened in 1976, subsequently capturing five of ECO's top exhibitions plus Terry Golding, previously financial director of ECO and now NEC chief executive. The five included the Motor Show and the important Furniture Show. Stewart-Smith shut Olympia's newest but least occupied Empire Hall after the Ideal Home Show in 1978, leasing it to a furnishing retailer as a superstore. Ideal Home was forced to move to Earls Court to regain the lost space. David Fasken replaced the Motor and Furniture Shows with strong variants, the hugely popular London Motorfair having first to overcome powerful objections from the ever-protective SMMT. It differed from their Motor Show in admitting dealer-exhibitors, thereby enabling visitors to place orders on the stand rather than back home. Regular auctions in the hall attracted large audiences for desirable machinery, and special features each year included displays of rare types, racing and record-breaking cars.

Cats, frocks and travel at Olympia

The Festival of Mind and Body at Olympia was launched in 1976 and ran on into the 1980s. 'Spirit' was added to the title in 1979. Exhibitors ranged from palmists and astrologers to the Catholic Society for the Protection of Feral Cats. One could marvel

Judgement day at the always crowded National Cat Show, Olympia, 1989. *(ECO)*

at Jeremy Lord's 'Bio-Activity Translator', a floral orchestra of weeds, flowers and microphones which synthesised the electrical impulses of plant life, turning them into mushy sound. The hippy 'Enlightodrome' offered a more contemplative alternative with the music of Steve Hillage, while the Scandinavian Yoga Centre offered a nose-clean. The popular aerobics programme included a 'taxi drivers' day'. It was all harmlessly entertaining and the media could be sure of finding a story on a quiet news day.

The National Cat Show, a one-day event at Olympia, was for years the world's largest following of the fancy. Attendances invariably reached the National Hall's licensed limit by mid-morning. Mrs Grace Pond put the whole show together alone and with great efficiency for over thirty-five years since bringing it to Olympia in 1956. Typically, 2,208 cats were shown in 1978. A hot-selling item on the stalls that year was a Japanese clockwork mouse.

The fashion industry swoops like a homing peacock on some novel platform for its collections and perches for a while, transforming it with colour and vibrancy before flying on. It could turn a locomotive shed into a chic salon if so minded. Olympia's London Fashion Exhibitions

Dog-tired. Crufts Dog Show, Earls Court, 1985. *(ECO)*

Prime Minister Margaret Thatcher meets models at the British Designer Show, Olympia, *c.* 1983. Organiser Joanne Davis is behind her. *(Joanne Davis)*

(later renamed the British Designer Shows) were in vogue for some ten years from 1976 in the most volatile of all event sectors. David Fasken's Philbeach Events Ltd, the exhibition-organising arm of ECO, captured the flighty industry in a series of superbly presented shows organised by Australian Joanne Davis, a no-nonsense professional with a knack for calming half-crazed couturiers on opening mornings. She went on to become deputy chief executive at Hong Kong's marble and glass Convention and Exhibition Centre. Joanne's colleague Caroline Cousins recalls a near-disaster at the first show. The iron roof of Grand Hall had expanded in the great heatwave of 1976 which ended with torrential rain the evening before the show opened. Swathed in acres of muslin, the roof leaked badly. If garments were not protected all hell would follow. Riggers fitted polythene sheeting beneath the muslin and sandbags on the surrounding gallery collected the discharge – just in time.

World Travel Market was the fastest-growing of any exhibition to pass through ECO. Its modest 1980 launch in Olympia's National Hall by organiser Frank Boiteaux of Reed Exhibitions brought a very satisfactory 7,753 trade buyers to see 350 exhibitors

Tom Nutley, organiser of World Travel Market. Launched in Olympia's National Hall in 1980, the show later outgrew even the Earls Court centre. *(Reed Exhibitions Ltd)*

Diana, Princess of Wales is greeted by Leonard Pearcey at the World Travel Market, Olympia, 1985. *(Reed Exhibitions Ltd)*

Chris Eubank successfully defends his WBO middleweight title against the elegant Gary Stretch at a sell-out match, Olympia, April 1991. (ECO)

from 46 countries. Twenty-one years on, at Earls Court, its 21,945 buyers were confronted with 4,763 exhibiting companies from 172 countries. The imperturbable Tom Nutley soon took it over and now also directs a clutch of satellite travel trade shows overseas.

WTM has had its little problems. When Taiwan first took a stand and put its flag on the fascia the Republic of China threatened to withdraw from the show. With a diplomatic incident in the making, Nutley moved fast to restore peace. Entertainment director Leonard Pearcey, producer of WTM's colourful in-hall stage shows since the launch, once devised a 'Children of the World' setting with costumed youngsters around a giant cushion bearing their national flowers. Nepal's emblematic plant entailed a high-altitude climb for a rare Himalayan species. Four flowers were picked. Two survived the descent and were flown to London. As they were reverentially woven into the cushion – the Dutch boy ate his tulip. On other occasions parrots have been absent without leave in the roof and a Texan armadillo had to be parked at London zoo between shows to meet quarantine regulations.

Pearcey sees each travel-themed production on his several stages as a live, three-dimensional tourism brochure. After a cautious initial reaction, demand for performance slots among nearly 200 countries is now his greatest headache. The pool at Earls Court was a godsend.

Trials and triumph

The industrial disputes that were a routine feature of national life culminated in the appalling 1978/9 'Winter of Discontent'. As Prime Minister James Callaghan's government contemplated a state of emergency in response to strike-hit petrol and coal supplies, diminishing food in the shops, rail strikes and the rest, the Transport & General Workers Union blacked the January Boat Show in a national dispute totally unrelated to the event or its industry. The show had suffered before. When the three-day week ruling in 1974 required it to remain closed without electricity for days at a time, ECO's Leslie Overs persuaded Board of Trade officials that running the show with only half the hall lights on daily would burn no more power than full lighting for two three-day periods. As this meant no power or lighting for the build-up in the windowless hall, stands were erected under car headlights and painters worked with a brush in one hand and a torch in the other.

The consequences this time could devastate the next inbound show, the author's British International Toy Trade Fair with 23,000 sq. metres of stands, filling Earls Court. It was the first big show to leave the NEC in preference for London and this was to be its debut in the capital. At twelve days' notice the organisers of both exhibitions learned from a bitter Ralph Carver, ECO's managing director, that the Boat Show would not be leaving the hall. Transport Union drivers refused to operate cranes to lift the boats out of the pool and to drive the trucks to clear them from the hall. The British Toy Fair generated nearly half the industry's annual sales worldwide. Without it many smaller manufacturers would not survive. In spite of representations to the union it was adamant. The British toy industry was expendable.

The author discusses his options with ECO commercial director David Coulson. The British International Toy Fair was denied access to set up at Earls Court during a national strike of transport workers in the 'Winter of Discontent', January 1979. (ECO)

The Boat Show managed to manhandle equipment from its upper floors to let the Toy Fair in there. Organisers, hall management and contractors worked round the clock to get 250 mostly big purpose-built stands reallocated from Earls Court's ground floor to Olympia's providentially empty Grand and Empire Halls. The Toy Fair opened on time, with a coach shuttle operating between the two halls. Earls Court's pool turned smelly and green while Olympia froze. There was no heating oil and drivers refused to deliver. In freezing daytime temperatures exhibitors wore overcoats; a large German group had brought food parcels over with their equipment. Industrial action had forced the cancellation of eight ECO exhibitions between 1969 and 1972, but Great Britain plc hit bottom that winter.

Tim Harris, dynamic ECO chairman and MD who secured funding for the £100m Earls Court 2. (The Times)

Sunseeker's stand at the London Boat Show in the stunning Earls Court 2 hall, 1991. (ECO)

The ending of the closed shop and other restrictive practices in the 1980s coincided with an explosion in the number and size of the UK's exhibitions. It marked a decade of astonishing growth at the two London centres and the NEC. The Empire Hall was retrieved, refitted, renamed Olympia 2 and relaunched in 1983 as a specialist exhibition venue. It booked twenty-two shows within days of the announcement. A conference centre was added soon afterwards. In a dramatic move in 1985 Sterling Guarantee merged with P&O and Jeffrey Sterling became chairman of the shipping construction, property and services giant. Chief accountant Tim Harris at ECO had risen through managing director to become chairman and MD. The incisive and hard-driving Harris finished what Stewart-Smith had begun. He initiated the £100 million Earls Court 2 hall.

The new hall (EC2) was badly needed to increase Earls Court's exhibition space and avoid driving super-shows such as the World Travel Market up to Birmingham. The striking new barrel-roofed hall which links with EC1 via folding shutters is large enough to hold four jumbo jets. The project was directed by Brigadier H. 'Rush' Dray, Earls Court's hall director, site-managed by P&O Developments' Geoff Taylor and built by Bovis Construction to the design of Kenneth Feakes of architects RMJM London Ltd. Feakes' design was inspired by St Pancras station. Clarke Nicholls and Marcel engineered the immense 275ft clear-span roof, thought to have been the world's

Bentley Boys! Earls Court's team of traffic controllers, 1980. Left to right: Frank Lear, Bert Southgate, George Pople at the wheel, Bert Wragge, Alf Sallis and Andy Murphy. *(Tony Hawkins)*

widest single-span structure. The hall's 17,000 sq. metre floor is entirely column-free. Over half the enormous cost went into the concrete base supported on 370 columns above the West London Railway and London Underground lines. The columns are positioned to allow for a possible future motorway. This 25,000 sq. metre platform with its service road is immensely strong: 45-ton Chieftain tanks can safely drive into the hall. EC2 was opened by Diana, Princess of Wales on 17 October 1991 for Motorfair.

Jam sandwich

'Life and Leisure' will never be forgotten by Olympia's old hands or, for sure, by the tens of thousands of members of the Women's Institute who came to Olympia for six days in the summer of 1984. The National Federation of the WI took over Grand Hall to present a vast exhibition demonstrating the broadening of interests of members as well as health and leisure opportunities and, they promised, 'half a mile of jam'. An entire village square with an operational village hall competed with continuous stage shows of folk dancing, street theatre and fashions. It was opened by the Queen, herself a WI member since 1943, and was great fun, though at the end of each long and noisy day several people found themselves stranded after missing their coaches home. Olympia staff helped them find transport or accommodation.

The Arabian desert came to Olympia in 1986 – tons of it. Saudi Arabia shipped sand over to cover part of the Grand Hall for a Bedouin encampment complete with date palms, camels, goats, a sheik's tent filled with rugs, silver and dark furniture and hooded

Impresario Harvey Goldsmith who introduced splendid opera to mass audiences at Earls Court. *(The Times)*

Carmen at Earls Court, 1989. The production had a cast of 500 and attracted nightly audiences of 11,000. *(ECO)*

falcons at the threshold, in a striking summer display of contrasting aspects of the country. An immense suspended tent-like dome 100ft across and 50ft high carried a panoramic image of modern Riyadh, clever lighting bringing a realistic and haunting dawn-to-dusk cycle every fifteen minutes as the commentary ran. Admission was free and buses toured London to shuttle the many visitors there and back, courtesy of the desert kingdom.

Harvey Goldsmith's opera

A cycle of grand opera began at Earls Court in 1988 with *Aida*, on a scale and before an audience greater than any previous production. Harvey Goldsmith's courageous – even visionary – gamble in mounting Giuseppe Raffa's £3m production for a three-performance run caused *The Times* to reflect that it made the Albert Hall look like a studio theatre. Grace Bumbry and Ghena Dimitrova were among the many fine soloists heading a cast of 600. The vast tiered set provided four acting platforms connected by moving stairways. Décor was projected in infinitely changing images to make a stunning backdrop.

The 499 extras, all unpaid volunteers, were rewarded with two free tickets, a certificate, a programme with their name inside (not in alphabetical order), free soft drinks and a contract prohibiting smoking or eating in costume, drink or drugs before performances and sunglasses on stage. Reviews ranged from 'pure magic . . . no serious harm was done to Verdi' to 'like eavesdropping on a neighbour playing a bootleg mono'. The audience loved it and Goldsmith returned the next year with *Carmen*, a splendid *Tosca* in 1991 and *Aida* again in 1998. 'Popera' it may have been, but Kiralfy and Cockie would have been delighted that it packed every performance and pleasurably introduced thousands to opera.

Dire Straits in concert, Earls Court, June 1992. *(ECO)*

Fireworks and farewells

Pop – the real thing – has filled Earls Court for years with audiences of up to 20,000. The roll of honour has included among many others Pink Floyd (1973), Genesis (1977), Bob Dylan (1981), Neil Diamond (1984), Peter Gabriel (1987), George Michael (1988), Dire Straits (1992), Def Leppard (1992), Elton John (1993), Oasis (1997), Eric Clapton (1998) and Madonna (2001). Neil Diamond returned in 2002.

Special effects requested by the producers of the Pink Floyd concert in 1973 included the burning of

USSR Exhibition, Earls Court, 1968. The show was lavish but strangely lifeless. *(ECO)*

an astronaut (refused as the sprinklers would be activated), and the firing of six rockets from the stage, over the audience to the Warwick Road end – approved subject to a sign being stuck to every seat beneath them reading: 'At the end of the Show flaming rockets will be projected on wires directly above your heads – THERE IS NO DANGER, DO NOT BE ALARMED.'

Prince's run of seven nights in 1992 was extended for two more to prevent West London going into gridlock as thousands of fans continued to swarm into the area in the hope of late tickets. The audience at an Oasis concert in 1995 stamped with such appreciation that reports of an earthquake tremor reached Scotland Yard from households up to a mile away. Every entrance into EC1 was effectively soundproofed with a second set of doors in 1993 in deference to the neighbours.

The 40th anniversary of the Queen's reign in 1992 was celebrated with a superb and at times hilarious pageant of the period in EC2 attended by Her Majesty and the Duke of Edinburgh, most of the royal family, the Prime Minister and Leader of the Opposition, parliamentarians of both houses and the great and good. Major Sir Michael Parker, the master of so many Royal Tournaments, devised and produced the show which, to almost everyone's delight, ran to twice its planned length.

Sir Michael Parker is emphatically in the Kiralfy tradition. No collective noun is safe in his keeping without a qualifying adjective. Bands are 'massed', choirs are 'immense', processions are 'vast', or occasionally 'vast and enormous'. Fireworks, his special delight, must be balletic – and ballistic – aerial conflagrations (friends allege he has twice

Auditioning youngsters at Olympia for *Bugsy Malone*. Director Mickey Dolenz chats to one hopeful among the 10,000 who turned up for one of the 96 parts on offer in February 1983. (*The Times*)

By 3pm the queue of youngsters for parts in *Bugsy Malone* snaked for a quarter of a mile round Olympia in icy weather. Fiona Hughes, twelve, from Loughborough was first in the queue at 4am with her father. A dawn snowstorm persuaded the promoters to let early arrivals into the warmth of the hall. All 10,000 were auditioned, boys of twelve in Chicago double-breasted chalk stripes and little misses of ten or so in leotards. First the basics, in groups of twenty, each sang 'Happy Birthday' and went through a simple dance routine. As Eric Watson, the rehearsal pianist, sucked raw fingers he calculated he would play the wretched tune 1,000 times. Survivors went on to sing 'You Give a Little Love' which was accompanied by more complex movements. Failures received a *Bugsy* badge and a Mars bar. (*The Times*)

Galloping hooves, chinking harness, glitter of wheels – and danger. The Kings Troop's unforgettable Musical Drive at the Royal Tournament, 1987. (ECO)

Olympia's heavy gangers, 1986. Left to right: Dave Penman, Jimmy Watson, Peter Turner and Henry Allen, with friends. (ECO)

RE-CYCLING AT OLYMPIA

narrowly avoided burning down Buckingham Palace). When planning the Royal Tournament at Earls Court Sir Michael once told the author, who was then hall director and rather concerned to keep the building standing, that he had an idea for the finale which involved a 54-tonne Chieftain bridge-laying tank throwing its bridge right across the arena. We concluded that this might prove rather too trying for the crew as the machine simultaneously descended through two floors on to the District Line below.

The Royal Tournament's last season in 1999 was a sell-out at every performance. And there it ended, a victim of defence spending cuts and government decree. It had been an annual focus of national pride, pageantry and sheer fun which generations held dear, not least the many visitors from abroad who also greatly enjoyed it.

That same year P&O announced an asset disposal programme. It was intended to raise more than £2 billion and free the P&O group to focus on its maritime activities. Earls Court and Olympia were up for sale.

Thanks first to an oil crisis and to Jeffrey Sterling's determined reaction, London's landmark halls have been more than turned around since 1972. A transformation united the old rivals, brought the halls to continental standards of service and performance, increased letting space to 100,000 sq. metres and achieved annual occupancy levels at record highs. Above all, the shows in their infinite variety from so many contributors continue to please and profit the two million people who visit them each year, and to give quiet satisfaction to the many men and women who work behind the scenes at Earls Court and Olympia. Without them all, the halls would fall dark.

There were many bidders, but it was very fitting that the outcome brings their story back full circle to Islington's Agricultural Hall, the senior of the trio in age if not size. The Morris family, who had successfully revitalised and relaunched it as the Business Design Centre, now completed the hat-trick to become the new owners of Earls Court and Olympia. All three halls were united at last.

TEN

SNAPSHOTS

Olympia International Show Jumping Championships

The first known show jumping contest was held in Paris in 1866 at a harness event. The riders did a little show in front of the stands and then disappeared across country over the obstacles. Understandably, the audience found this somewhat distancing. The following year all the jumps were put into the arena and a sport was born. A show jumping class took place at the first International Horse Show to be staged in England, at Olympia in 1907. As the sport gained in popularity it became clear that the many competitions lacked discipline and universal rules. A meeting was arranged at Olympia in 1923, and the British Show Jumping Association was formed in 1925.

The first Olympia International Show Jumping Championships was held in 1972 in the Grand Hall. Its timing just before Christmas was sheer luck – the Poultry Show had filled that slot until fear of fowl pest killed it off the year before. For the first three years Dunhills were lead sponsors. They invested start-up money and withdrew when the show began to break even. In salute to their steadfast support their dark red and gold house colours remain today. The Championships has become a premier competition attracting top international riders. Each year over 60,000 people watch 400 horses and 800 riders take part in a programme of international-standard events. As *The Times* puts it: 'The show is an agreeable blend of serious competition, pageantry, animal tricks and clowning around.' It has a festive flavour, the Christmas finale always closing with the arrival of Santa Claus in a mercifully brief blizzard to wild applause.

The Championships in its present form was created by Raymond Brooks-Ward in 1971. Raymond was something of a Harvey Goldsmith of his day. He wanted to create a show for children, specifically his children. And it has indeed become something of a family business. When the show started, camel racing was also part of the event. Ted

Christmas, and a box at the Olympia International Show-jumping Championships, 1987. *(ECO)*

Edgar, known as the Colonel of the Camel Corps, would regularly take a group of unwieldy camels along Kensington High Street to promote the show and with them, in fancy dress costume, went Raymond's young son James, along with twin Simon and younger brother Nick. This early experience obviously made an impression. James now heads the business development team at EC&O's Clarion Events, which owns and operates the show. Since the death of father Raymond, son Simon runs the production side and Nick is the commentator.

The show has a distinctive identity and rock-solid loyalty inside and outside the arena. Spectators who came as children now bring their own, and the offspring of competitors are now starting to jump too, including the famous Whittaker and Stewart clans. Pure magic.

London Book Fair

The Book Fair at Olympia is Europe's major spring publishing event. Established in 1971, it attracts a total audience of over 22,000 publishers and booksellers from around the world. They come to see the 1,200 companies exhibiting at the Fair or the 370 firms in its International Rights Centre where book, film, TV and translation rights are bought and sold. The Fair's sectors include publishing houses of all sizes, academic texts, children's books, travel books, art, architecture and design titles, religious books, remainder and promotional titles and service providers for publishing and book-selling.

As well as the serious business on the stands, seminars cover the latest issues and author events, publishing rights, retailing and e-business, allowing visitors and exhibitors

'The buzz' at the London Book Fair, Olympia, Europe's major spring publishing event. (Reed Exhibitions Ltd)

to catch up with news of the publishing world and, inevitably, the latest gossip. The 2002 Fair saw the launch of the first 'How to Get Published' event. Co-sponsored by the *Daily Mail* and WH Smith, it attracted an audience of over 400 members of the public, eager to listen to authors and experts from publishing. Speakers included best-selling writers Joanne Harris, Mike Gayle, Lisa Jewell and Magnus Mills. The new Readers and Writers Night, sponsored by the *Guardian* newspaper, Hay Festival and the Orange Prize for Fiction, was another successful addition to the programme and incorporated the popular Grand Author Party where 400 authors and their publicists gathered.

The Olympia Fine Art & Antiques Fairs

The first International Antiques Fair opened at Earl's Court on 18 March 1973, the debut of what are now thrice-yearly events. The *Antiques Trade Gazette* reported that the show had enjoyed a good start, and 'with a little tightening up' had every chance of becoming an annual event. Princess Margaret opened the 1974 Fair and became a regular visitor over the years. Another founding figure still associated with the Fairs is Leslie Weller, their chairman, as he is also of the vetting committees. He initially brought his expertise as an auctioneer (the first Fairs included daily auctions). Their high international standing is due in no small way to Leslie and Mrs Victoria Borwick, their director for many years.

The move to Olympia in 1976 brought a name change to the Fine Art & Antiques Fair. This was not the first such show at Olympia; in 1928, six years before the Grosvenor House Fair began, the very first antiques fair was staged there. Among the participants at that pioneering event were names still known in the trade today including Partridge, S.J. Phillips and Crowther, who still exhibit. The present Fair comprises pre-1830 works in the Gold section, more general stock or market items in the Silver section and items for a rummage in the Bronze area.

The organisers introduced two further fairs at Olympia, an Autumn Collectors Fair in 1990 and the Spring Fair which embraces home decoration in 1994. Memorable highlights include:

Who's driving? This mechanical elephant dating from the 1940s was accepted by the Olympia Fine Art & Antiques Fair as 'an item of exceptional interest'. *(Clarion Events Ltd)*

Emma Hallam (left) and Sarah Sutcliffe of the Fine Art & Antiques Fair direct the hoisting of a 750lb 3,000-piece chandelier for display at Olympia, 1999. *(The Times)*

- The launch of 'tarnish-free' silver. The nude paintings of pop queen Madonna in 2002. One of England's largest chandeliers ever exhibited, over 13ft tall. An antique pair of roller skates, ably demonstrated by Victoria Borwick.
- Loan exhibitions from Tibet and the Phoenician period; leading British artists such as Bacon and previously unknown works by John Constable, Edward Burra, Augustus John and his sister Gwen John.
- A life-sized mechanical elephant, dating from the 1940s, allowed into the Fair as 'an item of exceptional interest'.
- A unique collection of costumes, designed by Erté for a Parisian nightclub before the Second World War and modelled by Prima Ballerina Darcey Bussell.

The most expensive item ever shown at Olympia was a giant eighteenth-century silver wine cooler the size of a bath, which was bought for the nation by the National Art Collections Fund and exhibited at Olympia prior to taking its place in the Victoria & Albert Museum.

Over £60 million worth of business is done at the three Fairs each year, and Olympia is now acknowledged to be the 'barometer of the trade'. The last few years have seen further change since Andrew Morris bought EC&O. His vision for the Fairs led to a spectacular contemporary redesign and expansion of the Summer Fair in 2002, enthusiastically received by the public and dealers alike.

International Direct Marketing Fair

Like many good ideas that were turned into highly successful exhibitions, the International Direct Marketing Fair began life modestly. The inaugural show in 1977 was spread across fourteen table tops in the original Quaglino's Restaurant in London's West End. At Earls Court it is now one of the world's biggest marketing events attracting around 300 exhibitors and 12,000 visitors. Direct marketing as a technique has broadened from the envelope to e-mail, the telephone to the mobile and now to the website, with the postman's delivery the final link. The whole chain, including design services, specialist print, data capture services and the trade bodies, is built into the show, and its systems ensure that for better rather than worse, future customers can be more clearly identified and more appropriately reached.

Interestingly, the exhibition moved to Earls Court in 2003 for its silver jubilee event after two years at the impressive new ExCel centre in Docklands. The decision was taken in response to customer reaction – they wanted a West End venue. *Plus ça change . . .*

The BRIT Awards

Owned by the British Phonographic Industry (BPI), the trade association of British record companies, the BRIT Awards is now the leading and highest-profile music event in the UK entertainment calendar. Well known for its spectacular sets and controversial moments, the BRIT Awards is more than a television show, it is a major music event in

ts own right. Some 4,000 guests from the world of music and associated industries are entertained for dinner. A further 1,300 guests sit in the balconies and another 700 are in the 'pit', with 1,500 crew and artists working on-stage and backstage to create the annual celebration of British and international music.

First held at Wembley Conference Centre in 1977 as the British Record Industry Awards to mark the Queen's Silver Jubilee, the event then disappeared until it was staged at the Grosvenor House Hotel in 1982. Named the BRIT Awards in 1989, it first arrived at Earls Court in 1996. The show was hosted by Chris Evans and celebrated the music of its time with memorable performances from Michael Jackson, Pulp, Simply Red and Alanis Morisette. Original boy band Take That gave their farewell performance and David Bowie received an award for Outstanding Contribution to Music. Pulp lead singer Jarvis Cocker hit the headlines when he decided to make an unscheduled arrival on stage during Michael Jackson's performance of 'Earth Song'.

After a two-year break the BRIT Awards returned to Earls Court in 2000. Aficionados point to memorable moments ranging from 'Ginger Spice' Geri Halliwell's infamous Union Jack dress to the performance of cartoon band Gorillaz 'live' on stage, and some equally lively off-stage happenings from the likes of Jarvis Cocker and Chumbawamba's Danbert Nobacon. If this leaves you baffled, dear reader, you may care to tune in to the next show and check out the papers afterwards. The BRIT Awards has certainly come up with entertainment that makes headlines in the morning.

More 'buzz'. The Deutsche Post stand at the International Direct Marketing Fair. *(Reed Exhibitions Ltd)*

Monkeying with music –– Gorillaz cartoon band in concert, opening the BRIT Awards 2002 at Earls Court. *(BRIT Awards Ltd)*

What is less well known is that each year profits from the event are donated to good causes via the British Record Industry Trust, which was established in 1989 to encourage young people in the exploration and pursuit of educational, cultural or therapeutic benefits deriving from music. The main beneficiaries are the BRIT School for performing arts and technology (the only non-fee-paying performing arts school in the country) and Nordoff-Robbins Music for music therapy.

Amusement Trades Exhibition International

It may be an awkward title but the ATEI is the name of the game in the gaming industry. This glittering and strictly trade-only Earls Court show vibrates with electronic sound effects from a thousand slot machines, overlying a murmur of deal-making at the world's largest exhibition for the amusement trades. The show began in 1936 and came to Olympia in 1981. It now comprises the Amusement Trades Exhibition

International, covering coin-operated products and services, the International Casino Exhibition and the Visitor Attractions Show launched in 2002 for the UK tourism sector. Exhibitors from some 115 nations and over 14,000 visitors attend the impressively well-organised show. Exhibits range from regulation playing cards to coin-slot and pinball games, air hockey, plush gaming tables and the latest hi-tech robots.

Among the show's most fervent supporters is an Australian exhibitor who wrote:

Serious money at the Amusement Trades Exhibition International, Earls Court. The world's largest show for the amusement trades hosts exhibitors from 115 countries and attracts over 14,000 visitors each year. *(ATE)*

The Christmas period through January in Australia is as close as many of us will ever get to Heaven: magnificent summer weather, some of the best sporting events you will ever see, barbecues and ice cold beer with family and friends around the pool. . . . Yet each year, for more than I really want to remember, I dig out the overcoat, scarf and gloves, pack the old grip and leave Heaven behind. I jump on a Jumbo for a 30-hour ride to spend a week in London where the beer is warm, the pools are iced over, and the weather is foul. . . . I learned a long time ago that if you're working in the amusement industry there's only one place to be in late January and that's ATEI.

As with every trade fair, the show is a sounding board for its industry, the state of its health, its concerns, output and performance. ATEI enables politicians and the media to see the best of Britain's gaming and gambling sector.

FRESH START
by Andrew Morris

WHEN I WALK THROUGH THE DOORS of Earls Court and Olympia I often still catch my breath. These two grand old ladies of London are so much more than just empty halls filled each week with a different show or event. They are blank canvases and each show organiser is the artist. They are meeting places alive with people who are seeing something new, doing important deals or just plain having fun. And, as this book has demonstrated so vividly, these buildings are also monuments to the billions of people and thousands of shows that make up the collective history of Earls Court and Olympia. When the halls are empty and it's quite dark and still, you can hear echoes of shows from the past and if you look harder you can imagine those still to come. I feel a tremendous sense of pride and responsibility in my role at the helm of this company. But getting here has been a tough and exhilarating ride.

The story begins on 24 March 1999. Two things conspired to happen on that day that changed not only my life but the whole exhibitions industry. Firstly the team behind the new challenger in East London, ExCel, announced that it had finally secured funding, and secondly, having shown us the door two years previously, shipping company P&O finally announced their intention to focus on their core business of shipping and to sell Earls Court and Olympia.

Andrew Morris, Chief Executive, Earls Court & Olympia Group. *(ECO)*

My father Sam Morris began our family business in 1954 with a five-pound note and a smart idea, and took the Morris family from Billingsgate fish market, where he was a porter, to the Business Design Centre in Islington in the years that followed. The company, City Industrial Limited, grew from modest beginnings to a respectable size over three decades and by the time the sales sign went up at Earls Court and Olympia, I'd been running the Business Design Centre for thirteen years since it opened its doors in October 1986.

Together with my brother Jack we'd created a niche five-star venue in a new part of town for the exhibitions industry. I needed a fresh challenge and

seized on this new opportunity. In my mind this was the prize job in the industry in the most important venues in the UK. Having cut my teeth in a small venue I was ready for the big one.

The sale was to be by closed auction, a management buy-out having been quickly ruled out by the P&O board. The style of management in those days was very hierarchical and formal and was memorably described as being 'in aspic' – wonderfully preserved. Little changed year on year and there was negligible investment in either the venues or the people who ran them. Change was badly needed.

Having discussed things with the family, Jack and I decided to step away from our day-to-day roles at the Business Design Centre to give this our all. Our first step was to appoint M&A consultants, Livingstone Guarantee Trust, in the shape of Tim Lyle. Tim was there to protect the Morris family's interests because my father began – and his five sons continue to build – this company for future generations and it was critical that we got this huge undertaking right. Following a beauty parade of venture capitalists our next appointment was Candover Investments, who were chosen for their success rate on deals rather than the volume. Their pedigree is impeccable and their dedication impressive. Simon Leefe led the deal and is a valued member of the board of EC&O Group to this day.

There were about seventy other prospective buyers, but gradually the numbers were whittled down by various selection processes until only two or three companies were left in the last round. It was a great adventure. There was intrigue at every turn. Who were our rivals? What was our next step? We had never undertaken anything like this and so each day brought a new challenge and a steeper learning curve. Competition was fierce and we used all our resources, wit and collective wisdom to keep ourselves in the game.

Our reporting accountants were Ernst & Young. They sent along a young numbers man called Tim Pilcher who set up camp with us in our cramped offices throughout the six months. So impressed were we not just with his financial acumen but with his character and intellect that, following our successful purchase, we invited him to come in-house and join us as Financial Director. Mention should also be made of John Dunford, Tim's colleague at Ernst & Young, Tina Williams of Fox Williams and also Chris Hale of Travers Smith Braithwaite, all of whom should be honoured for their efforts to help us win this most challenging of business deals.

After six months work we heard that in principle the deal was done. The date was Wednesday 29 September 1999. The P&O legal team met with our team at 5pm and discussions went on through the night. We slept in reception, not daring to move for fear we'd miss something. Thursday came and went and the deal slowly came together. Finally, at 7pm, it came to signing the papers. I had just started to make a speech of thanks when Hugh Scrimgeour, chairman of ECO, interrupted me. He wanted to speak first, as is the prerogative of the seller and he spoke with great dignity.

And so then it was done. It was Friday 1 October 1999 and I was to be the new chief executive of Earls Court & Olympia Group with Jack taking up a non-executive role on the board. This was a shared victory, but it was more than a little sad as it meant that Jack and I would no longer work closely together. We'd had little contact with the staff of the two venues through the process, but we knew that they had to be our first priority. The sale of a company is inevitably a traumatic ordeal for those who work there. So while we were desperate to hit the Friday media deadlines for Saturday's papers, first we had to talk to our new team. After a wash and brush up, at 10.30 on that Friday I took the floor, in front of some 750 employees, as the new Chief Executive of Earls Court and Olympia.

It was a remarkable gathering. Hugh Scrimgeour introduced me and I took the stage in front of a sea of new faces, all with very different expectations of me but united in their desperate need to learn their fate and that of their company. They were utterly silent and attentive and I knew that I had to get not only the words but also the tone right, because this first impression would stick for years to come. So I told them what I had to tell them about changes to the business, but focused most of my speech on giving them an insight into the Morris family, the way we work and our values – because ultimately I believe that people trust people, not structures.

I remember telling them that we had taken over a great company – a company made great because of them. I stressed that I had been impressed with the dedication, intelligence and professionalism of those that I'd already met and that I expected great things from them all. To hear the challenge 'everyone has a creative side – we want to see yours' must have been surprising after twenty-five years of the patriarchal P&O. But, as the years have passed, I hope that I have been as good as my word and given everyone in the business the chance to bring creativity to their roles.

I spent the rest of the Friday doing interviews. A celebratory party had been arranged in an Islington restaurant, Granita, and it was also to be my farewell bash as the following Monday I would take up my new post. At midnight Jack, my wife Jennifer and I sneaked away from the celebrations to go to King's Cross station where we picked up the first editions and read our story. Then it was straight back to the BDC to pack up my desk. Hugh Scrimgeour moved out of his office on the fourth floor of Earls Court on Saturday 2 October and I lugged my boxes in on the Sunday morning.

I remember driving a very packed four-wheel-drive down Earls Court Road with Nicola Pugh, a member of my team who, along with Nigel Nathan (soon to be commercial director of EC&O Group), had come with me from the BDC. I spotted an *Evening Standard* 'A-board' advertising the headline 'Earls Court and Olympia sold'. 'Get that for me' I said to Nicola, and she hopped out of the car. I imagined that she'd offer the vendor some money and so got my wallet ready . . . but a few seconds later she jumped breathless into the car with the whole A-board in her arms and shouted at me to 'DRIVE!' The whole thing, metal frame and all, is now hung on my office wall. Somewhere though there must be a very annoyed *Evening Standard* vendor and I'd like to put on the record my apologies for the outrageous snatch and grab!

I took up my new post on Monday 4 October 1999, exactly thirteen years to the day since we'd opened the doors of the Business Design Centre for the first time. If anyone asks me what my lucky date is – then it would have to be that one. The emotion, the trauma, the stress and the exhaustion involved in both of those enterprises has proven worth it by any measure in each case. So now we had it – our business deal was done. But the hard work was far from over – in fact it was only just beginning.

The first ninety days in any new business venture are critical. Our first step was to focus the company on doing what we felt we could do best, which is running exhibition venues. P&O had created a number of service operations within the company such as catering, audio-visual, contracting, etc. We out-sourced or sold these fairly swiftly to leading companies in each field so that we could concentrate on playing to our strengths. As a result our directly employed staff went from 750 to 250 in six months – but many of the staff who worked in these service areas stayed on in the buildings with their new employers as 'service partners', and are still a valuable part of the wider team.

Our new approach was customer-focused. P&O had adopted a landlord–tenant approach with customers and we knew that we had to win exhibition organisers over – and do it quickly because the clock was ticking down to the opening of ExCel. The business was not competitive. We had to change that, and fast.

We embarked upon a £60m refurbishment programme, designed to transform the buildings and make them more flexible, attractive and well-equipped for the needs of show organisers. We also took a long hard look at exhibition catering, something that almost all our customers were united in their dislike of. We felt that if we couldn't do it impeccably ourselves then we should bring in the best of the high street concerns – which we did in the shape of Costa Coffee, Pizza Express, Soup Opera and Pret à Manger.

The whole board of the company changed in the first six months. Nigel and Tim had already started work with us and my next appointments were equally critical ones. First we brought in former Wembley and Dome operations expert Jon Sellins to head up the operational teams as Group Halls Director. Secondly we brought in the energetic powerhouse Simon Kimble to revolutionise our in-house organising company Clarion Events. We have also brought on board media industry expertise in the form of our chairman David Arculus, who helped to build both IPC and EMAP, and public affairs expert Des Wilson, formerly director of corporate and public affairs at BAA plc.

On my first day in the job I received a letter from Tom Nutley of World Travel Market – giving me the devastating news that the show was to move to ExCel. We'd planned for around a quarter of our shows to head east, but it was still a blow to lose such a high-profile event. The Boat Show soon followed suit, as did Hotelympia and, sure enough, over those first twelve months, around 25 per cent of our customers announced the intention to disappear off to Docklands. We were working long hours and, despite all the planning for ExCel, it was hard to watch the shows go, knowing that we were not yet ready to fight back. A desire to try something new is only natural, and we did not yet offer a realistic alternative.

That period was also the toughest time for me personally. One evening, when it was still early days, we were struggling to sell the stand catering and banqueting business and meetings were over for the Christmas break, I sat in my office. All was quiet and I don't think I have ever felt as lonely as I did at that moment. Although we had acquired a profitable business, great sites and a great brand, the under-investment was clearly visible, the employees were demotivated and insecure, customer service was poor and the inherited management style was archaic. In short, this was a turnaround situation but it was not going to happen overnight.

Skip on almost three years and the situation could not be more different. More than a dozen of those shows have come back to us, either because visitors made it clear that they preferred the shows to be located in our venues, or because organisers have been pleased with our efforts to transform Earls Court and Olympia. In addition we're winning new shows and, through Clarion, creating new launch ideas of our own. We have invested in a massive culture change programme with our staff to liberate the enthusiasm, passion and abilities that we know they have.

We know, from what customers and visitors are telling us, that the work we have done over the last three years is paying off. These two beautiful landmarks of London are still considered by many to be the best place to hold a show, with more visitors per square metre and bags of character to go with the new facilities and services that we have built to make sure we are competitive. We are working hard on our relationships with our local communities and are determined to be good neighbours as well as good exhibition venues.

So, what's next? Well, we can't rest on our laurels. We need to remain competitive because, while ExCel is struggling at the moment, it is a fantastic venue that has driven up standards in the industry and will ultimately find its market and prove to be a huge success. There are also opportunities to take the lessons and skills that we have learnt in London and use them to acquire or run other venues around the world.

But, ultimately, the biggest challenge remains in what is still to be achieved within the walls of Earls Court and Olympia. There are still gaps in our calendar to fill with new ideas, new shows and events and that's the fun of this business. The only limit is your imagination. Providing we keep an eye on how visitors want to spend their time, we can create shows for every niche, every business and every interest. How many chief executives get to do that every day?

INDEX

Numbers in **bold** indicate black and white illustrations, with or without accompanying text. Colour plates are not indexed.

EXHIBITIONS & ENTERTAINMENTS

GENERAL INDEX